Dear Caregiver, It's Your Life Too

71 Self-Care Tips To Manage Stress, Avoid Burnout & Find Joy Again While Caring For A Loved One

Katie Duncan

Nurse Practitioner

Contents

The Crucial Toolkit For End-Of-Life Care   ix

Introduction   xiii

How To Read This Book   xxiii

1. Tip #1   1
Get Organized

2. Tip #2   7
CATCHIN' Z's

3. Tip #3   11
Good M-ooor-ning!

4. Tip #4   13
Wash It Off

5. Tip #5   15
'Tooth' Be Told

6. Tip #6   17
Clean Clothes, Fresh Start

7. Tip #7   19
Fresh Nails

8. Tip #8   21
Eat Food

9. Tip #9   24
Drink, Drink, Drink... Water

10. Tip #10   27
"When You Gotta Go... Go!"

11. Tip #11   29
Exercise

12. Tip #12   32
Your Health & Medical Care

13. Tip #13   36
Practice Acceptance

14. Tip #14   38
Honor Your Choice

15. Tip #15   41
Steer Clear Of Perfection

16. Tip #16   44
Self Check-In

17. Tip #17   49
Be The Student

18. Tip #18   52
Ask Questions

19. Tip #19   54
Be The Parrot

20. Tip #20   56
Over Clarify

21. Tip #21   58
Write It All Down

22. Tip #22   60
Ask For Help

23. Tip #23   64
Learn To Say "Yes"

24. Tip #24   65
The Power Of "No"

25. Tip #25   68
Seek Out Your Resources

26. Tip #26   71
Appoint A Spokesperson

27. Tip #27   73
Designate An Accountability Partner

28. Tip #28   76
Get To Know Your Healthcare Support Team

29. Tip #29   78
Talk To A Pro'

30. Tip #30   80
Connect With People

31. Tip #31   83
Get Community Support

32. Tip #32   85
Use Respite Care

33. Tip #33   87
Try Meditation

34. Tip #34   91
Be Mindful

35. Tip #35   95
Remember To Breathe

36. Tip #36   98
A Good Morning Stretch

37. Tip #37   100
Brain Dump With A Journal

38. Tip #38   103
Practice Gratitude

39. Tip #39   106
Repeat Positive Affirmations

40. Tip #40   108
Reconnect With Your Identity

41. Tip #41   112
It's Time... It's "Me-Time"

42. Tip #42   115
Seek Financial Assistance

43. Tip #43   121
Seek Spiritual Support

44. Tip #44   123
Celebrate Small Wins

45. Tip #45   126
Be Your Own Best Cheerleader

46. Tip #46   128
Hire A Homecare Assistant

47. Tip #47   130
When In Doubt, Alert Your Care Team

48. Tip #48   131
Keep One Small Promise To Yourself

49. Tip #49   133
Set Up Boundaries

50. Tip #50   136
Forgive Yourself

51. Tip #51   137
Forgive Others

52. Tip #52   138
Get Into Nature

53. Tip #53   140
Let Go Of What Is Out Of Your Control

54. Tip #54   143
Put Effort Into What You Can Control

55. Tip #55   145
Don't Get Down On Yourself

56. Tip #56   148
Learn From Your Mistakes

57. Tip #57   150
Be Present, It's Truly A Present

58. Tip #58   155
When Things Get Hard... Keep Going!

59. Tip #59   158
   Respect Our Differences

60. Tip #60   160
   Divvy Up The Responsibilities

61. Tip #61   162
   Lookin' Fancy

62. Tip #62   164
   Treat Yourself

63. Tip #63   166
   Laugh Often

64. Tip #64   169
   Be Flexible

65. Tip #65   172
   The Power Of A Hug

66. Tip #66   174
   Detox

67. Tip #67   179
   Sexy Time

68. Tip #68   181
   I Believe

69. Tip #69   184
   Don't Wipe Away Those Tears

70. Tip #70   186
   Say Cheese

71. Tip #71   189
   Open Up Your Lens

   Conclusion   195

   Please Share   199

   BONUS   201

   Acknowledgments   203

   About the Author   205

   Also by Katie Duncan   207

   The Crucial Toolkit For End-Of-Life Care   209

72. References   211

THE CRUCIAL TOOLKIT FOR END-OF-LIFE CARE

Get Your Exclusive Copy Now!

In the Crucial Toolkit For End-Of-Life Care, you'll learn...

- The 7 most important medications used at the end-of-life and why

- The 4 most essential and easy to use templates to keep every caregiver organized
- The simplest guide to understanding your hospice professional team members
- The 5 best questions to ask your healthcare team when caring for someone at the end-of-life

Insert link in browser:

www.deathcarecoach.com

To all of you who dedicate yourselves to caring for others. I see you. I appreciate you.
You, too, deserve peace.
This is for you.

INTRODUCTION

"Self-care is never a selfish act – it is simply good stewardship of the only gift I have, the gift I was put on earth to offer others. Anytime we can listen to true self and give the care it requires, we do it not only for ourselves, but for the many others whose lives we touch."

- Parker J. Palmer

BEEP BEEP BEEP BEEP

Ugh.

You sleepily roll over in bed as you blindly reach for the bedside table. Then, moving your hand to the left, you tap the snooze button on your alarm. Oof. It's 6:00 a.m. on Saturday.

It's another day.

With your eyes shut, eyelids heavy, you attempt to move. First one leg, then the other, you shove them over the edge of the bed. Finally, you shift your hips as one hand pushes onto the mattress to force your body upright.

Well, yesterday was a day. It started with cleaning up her soiled bedding first thing in the morning. Quickly you forced breakfast into her and rushed out the door to her doctor's appointment. Of course, of all mornings, you forgot to give her medication, which her doctor reminds you is of "utmost importance." Getting her home and resituated back onto the couch took over an hour. You wanted to give up when there was nothing to feed her for dinner. When all was said and done, you finally got her into bed. She didn't fall asleep until after midnight, and, to top it off, she woke you up at 3:00 a.m. after falling out of bed trying to get to the toilet. Just another Friday, that was.

It felt like you had just winked when the alarm decided to go off. Vision blurry, you look up at the ceiling and passively think to yourself, "How long can I keep doing this?" Closing your eyes one last time, you take one slow deep breath in, holding it for just a second before letting it go.

Shoving the rest of the comforter off your side, you force your body to move. You slide the soles of your feet to the floor, feeling the soft carpet under your toes, and, in a daze, you stand.

Another day.

THE CAREGIVER ROLE

Having picked up this book, I assume you are currently caring for or preparing to care for a loved one, either full-time or part-time. This may be a short-term job, or this may be, or unknowingly turn into, a long-term job as you journey with them through the end of their life.

Some of you have been at this caregiving thing for quite a while now. Others of you may be just beginning. This job, the caregiver job, isn't for everyone. While it can be gratifying, caregiving can also be a winding, bumpy, confusing, frustrating, exhausting, isolating, lonely, and incredibly stressful job.

Most, if not all of us, found ourselves falling into this caregiver role unexpectedly and maybe even out of the blue. When we find ourselves here, we have no idea what to expect and what being a caregiver entails. We're often learning as we're going and just trying to get through it one day at a time.

Your loved one has Alzheimer's, Parkinson's Disease, or another form of Dementia. They've had a stroke or have another chronic disease like kidney failure or heart failure. They're disabled or have been aging and simply need more help.

All of us caregivers found ourselves in this role for some reason. Some of us may have felt obligated, as if we were forced into this role because our loved one had no one else.

Or...

We were the only daughter.
We were the spouse.
We were the parent.
We were the only ones who could drop our lives to be here.
We were the "responsible" child.
We were their closest friend.
Or we were some version of one of these.

Some of us may have felt like this was our duty – out of love, repayment, or responsibility. For some of us, taking on this caregiver role was our vocation. It aligned with our morals and values. And it gave us a sense of virtue, that we were following our purpose in life. And finally, for some of us, it may have felt like it was the only thing left to do. And now, in many ways, it feels like just another burden in our lives.

No matter how you came to this role, it takes an extraordinary person to be a caregiver, and you are one of them. All of us caregivers know, or will come to find out, this role is far from easy. In fact, it's quite the opposite of easy.

In addition to the responsibilities of *your* everyday life - your children, spouse or partner, job, finances, physical health, social life, hobbies, mental health, household chores, and the list goes on - you're also tending to the daily needs of your loved one. Being a caregiver often requires you and maybe others in your family to unexpectedly put your entire lives on hold. While everyone's situation looks different, you might be the one...

Bathing them.
Grooming them.
Helping them to the bathroom, bedside commode, and eventually changing their soiled diapers.
Washing their genital parts.
Cooking and feeding them.
Dressing them.
Walking, relocating, or repositioning them.
Giving them physical, mental, emotional, spiritual, and maybe even financial support.
Medicating them.
Managing their finances.
Managing their household chores.
Doing the transporting and shopping.
Communicating with family, friends, and others.
Arranging and updating their healthcare team.

Well, by golly!

That is a whole lot to be accountable for. And suppose you are caring for someone who once took care of you, such as a parent or grandparent. In this case, many of these things may feel very uncomfortable for you and maybe even them.

Throughout your caregiving journey, you will feel some level of pressure, tension, and weight. This is known as caregiver stress. Not even the most organized, prepared, and knowledgeable can completely escape it. The trick is to somehow find a way to stay healthy *and* sane by balancing your well-being, keeping you steady and stable.

As a nurse practitioner, a family member of ill and now deceased loved ones, a friend, and even a human, I've worn the caregiver hat many times. I know how exhausting, draining, lonely, and overwhelming it can feel. Coping with caregiver stress can be so challenging that we find ourselves teetering on the edge of complete burnout. I've felt burnout. It's awful, and I don't wish it on anyone, especially you, caregiver. And that is why I wrote this book: to help you cope with your emotions, manage your stress, and help you prevent caregiver burnout.

HOW?

From my experience, self-care has always been my saving grace. It has been *the* answer for myself and others as we've somehow found balance through the havoc of caring for those we love. Through exhaustion, overwhelm, and fatigue, self-care has been and continues to be the unsung hero that keeps our internal pressure from reaching the boiling point.

In this book, I offer self-care tips I have used in my personal caregiving experiences and tips my patients and families have shared with me. To help protect the privacy of others, I've changed names and genders within the stories I share. Many of these coping mechanisms are research-based and follow other health and wellness guidelines.

As simple as some of these tips may seem, these daily practices not only support but help maintain the *foundation* of your health and wellness. They are the habits that keep your body, mind, spirit, and soul in alignment.They are what keep you strong and sturdy, prepared and ready to prevent your own body from becoming sick or diseased.

You are only as strong as your foundation.

Choosing self-care is the responsible choice. These acts of self-love, self-compassion, and self-kindness will reveal your greatest self. So step into this new you and watch as you show up an even better caregiver.

FOR THE DOUBTER

Trust me, I know hearing the advice, "You've got to take care of yourself first," is something many of you will reject, maybe even scoff at.

"If one more person says to me 'make sure you are taking care of yourself, too,' I don't want to hear it."
"Take care of myself?!"
"Ha! That's just not going to happen."
"No one is going to convince me to put myself first and not a thing in the world will change my mind."
"How can you expect me to take care of myself right now?"
"Who do you think I am? My [loved one] is sick. And you expect me to think about *ME?*
"There isn't enough time in the day to do it all... especially anything for me."
"I *will not* leave them alone."
"No one, not even *you*, can convince me to leave their side, to rest, to take a shower, to exercise, to do anything but be with them right now."
"They need me."

....*Gently,* I am going to *pause* you right there because you're right.

They need you.

For me, these were the words that stuck. In the thick of my caregiving journey, my instinct was to throw a hand up at anyone who gave me that irritating self-care reminder. It was never going to click unless I was in the right head-space to allow myself to hear and understand it. While always heartfelt, the advice irked me until I heard those words. The realization finally hit me.

They needed me.

These words made that annoying advice finally penetrate the wall I had built around me. It was the "Aha!" moment I'd been needing without even knowing I needed it.

"This was it," I thought. "*I am it.* I am the one flying this plane. If I get sick, if I'm not in good mental and physical shape, if something happens to me, if I don't take care of myself, well that's it. This plane crashes and the whole thing falls apart."

For me, "*they*" have been many people - from my family, friends, and dying loved ones to my patients and their families. These were the words I needed to hear to finally acknowledge and appreciate that I needed to reprioritize myself, with "Me" plastered to the top of my priority list.

I needed to be unshakeable - body, mind, and spirit. Because if I wasn't, if I let myself drop from that #1 spot, if there was even a crack in my armor, I would not be able to provide *or* care for anyone else. I'd crash the plane. I'd sink the ship. I'd burn the house down along with everyone else inside. No one would get what they deserved. Not me. Not my loved ones. Not my family or friends. Not my patients or their families.

This is my *WHY*. This is why I make self-care my priority. And I hope you do, too. Because if you do not, it's not "if" but "when." You, too, will sink the ship with your loved ones on board. Sincerely from my heart, I hope this is your real, genuine, direct reminder that…

> *You can make time for yourself,*
> *and you must make time for yourself.*

Your loved one needs you. So if not for you, do it for them.

FOR SANITY

Some of you may have picked up this book for that exact reason.

> *Your sanity.*

You are struggling to find balance in your life – balancing not only your emotions but the emotions of others. Balancing not only your normal day-to-day and personal life but the caregiving responsibilities for your loved one. And maybe, above all, you are struggling to find balance within your whole self: the physical, mental, emotional, spiritual, social, financial, occupational, and environmental parts of you. These eight aspects make up your overall well-being, and some, if not all, are *not* doing well.

You feel hopeless. You need help. And you're desperate. You know you're about to reach your breaking point, and you're a pin drop away from the "point of no return." Well, my friend, you came to the right place.

FOR THE PROACTIVE

Some of you may be here because you took on this new or changing caregiver role and are aware of the stress that goes along with it. Maybe some of you have been in similar situations or have ideas about what's to come. Maybe some of you are "givers" or "caregivers" at heart in your day-to-day lives and understand the need for balance. You realize that when caring for someone you love, you give so much of yourself that you risk burning out. Regardless, you are here because you want to get ahead of the game so that you can better manage future stressors.

My friend, you too have come to the right place. Keep reading.

CAREGIVER STRESS & SELF-NEGLECT

Most of us can handle difficulty and hardship for a short time. We can adjust. Make changes. We learn to adapt and control what we can to make things easier for us. We find coping mechanisms to manage our stress, at least for the short term. But stress becomes chronic as we continue caring for our loved one for an unknown length of time. It never fully goes away.

Why?

Your loved one quickly becomes your #1 priority. You spend all your time and every bit of your energy caring and worrying about them. From taking extended time off work to spending less time with your spouse, children, and friends to forgetting to eat in the morning – it seems your whole life now revolves around your loved one. It can be confusing and difficult to separate this new role as a caregiver from other roles you identify: spouse, lover, parent, child, friend, and others.

While riding an emotional roller coaster and juggling the never-ending list of caregiving duties, you attempt to maintain your life. The new burdens, however, continue to rack up, and the stress begins to consume you. The stress often sneaks up on you, becoming exhausting and, quite honestly, tormenting. Unknowingly, you become so trapped in stress and transfixed in your caregiver mentality that it becomes your new identity. It becomes nearly impossible to think about *anything* or *anyone*, including yourself.

Before you realize it's happening, you stop taking care of *You*. You neglect *your* health, *your needs, and your* desires and quickly lose sight of your well-being. This self-neglect is damaging not only you but your loved one and maybe others in your life.

By allowing your well-being to take the backseat, you can never truly be at your best. When you are not your best self, you cannot care for your loved one as you both desire and deserve.

What I fear and have seen far too many times is what happens when that stress and self-neglect continue to go unnoticed, ignored, or unmanaged. There's only one thing left.

Burnout.

Young and old, healthy and diseased, single and married, parent and child. I have seen caregivers of all ages become suddenly unable to care for their ill or dying loved ones.

They've gotten sick.
They've had a fall or broken a bone.
They've ended up with debilitating depression.

They've lost their home.
They've had a heart attack or stroke.
They've ended up in the hospital.
And in the worst situations, they've ended up meeting death sooner than the loved one they had been caring for.

Dear Caregiver,

It is not *if* but *when*. And when that time comes, you will not be able to care for anyone, including your loved one. No one wants this for you. You don't want this for you. Your loved one doesn't want this for you. I don't want this for you. That is why I've dedicated this book to you. You *can* manage this stress. You can prevent yourself from reaching total burnout. It doesn't have to get that far.

Dear Caregiver,

You are kind. You are compassionate. You are a giver. But you are not invincible, and you don't have to be. Caregiving is indeed a selfless act, and I thank you for that. But it is self-care that is true selflessness.

Dear Caregiver,

You are deserving. You are worthy. And you are appreciated. It's time to show *Your-Self* the compassion, love, and grace that is so rightfully due.

How To Read
This Book

There is no right or wrong way to read this book. As you journey through this book, you will notice that many tips I share are quite simple. Some might even say common sense. However easy and obvious as they may seem, when you're deep in the thick of it all, it's hard to recognize what you are or are not doing and how those things affect you.

Some of you may read straight through this book in a day. You might be excited to start incorporating many of these tips into your daily life. Others may read one tip daily because it's easier to digest in small bites. Taking in too many tips at one time may feel overwhelming. You may feel uneasy, doubtful, or hesitant to integrate some or all of these tips into your life. If this is the case, when you come across a tip that feels manageable, try it out once to see how it feels. Whether you use a tip once or decide to continue it going, be proud that you are allowing yourself the opportunity to build your resilience.

Doing new things is never comfortable, but they help us learn, grow, evolve, and heal. As a result, we become better versions of ourselves, enabling us to deepen our connection with others. With this book, I invite you to give yourself that chance.

I am grateful for the opportunity to share these simple yet powerful practices to help keep you steady throughout your caregiving journey. If there is even one tip you take away from this book that positively impacts your life, then I call that a win because your well-being has no price tag.

TIP #1
GET ORGANIZED

"Good order is the foundation of all things."

- Edmund Burke

I SPENT time with a woman named Debra. Debra was the full-time caregiver for her mother, who was also dying of Alzheimer's. At the same time, she supported three adult children, grand-mothered eight busy grandchildren, and cared for her recently hospitalized spouse. In addition, several nights a week, Debra would work to bring in enough money to make ends meet.

Whenever I visited Debra, I thought, "Wow, how is she doing it all? How is she still standing?" One day I finally asked. She looked at me and just laughed.

She walked me into her kitchen, and there they were. Taking over the kitchen table were different colored binders for each person she cared for — her mother, each child and grandchild, her spouse, and even herself. Debra filled each binder with individual schedules, medication lists and logs, appointment reminders, and running to-do lists. Plastered on her refrigerator was a monthly calendar with pencil markings and different colored highlighters. Debra said, "This is how. This is the *only* way how."

———

Your caregiving duties can range from minimal to many, depending on your situation. Either way, with these major life changes and likely unfamiliar responsibilities, your body is just waiting to scream "stress overload!"

Organization is the key to combating this burden. Research suggests it reduces stress, improves sleep, and supports good eating habits. Additionally, it can help you stay productive and strengthen your relationships with those around you.

There are many ways to do this, and some might work for you better than others. To start, look around your home. What does your environment look like? Is your space clean? Is it messy? The space we live in is often a reflection of how we feel. It tells us what's really going on inside. For example, a messy home indicates we're in chaos. Whereas a clean home means we are calm and well-composed. Clearing your space will clear your mind, so go ahead and try the strategies mentioned later in this tip.

After organizing your home, think about ways to find order in your life. From schedules, calendars, and planners, to logs, records, check-lists, and alarms, use the following strategies to create a toolkit to keep you organized. While it may seem like a waste of your time, creating these tools now will save you more time in the future. Soon, they will turn into one of your greatest allies.

When new and old responsibilities add up, your memory bank becomes too overwhelmed to remember most things. As a result, you find yourself losing track of both day and time. Using these tools, you don't have to worry about remembering your growing list of obligations. You simply follow a plan. You can't forget when it's right in front of you.

STRATEGY #1

DECLUTTER YOUR SPACE

It's time to tidy up your environment. Clear out, reorganize, and simplify your living space to declutter your mind.

Technique #1

Work on cleaning and organizing one room at a time. My suggestion would be to start with the room you spend the majority of your time. When you finish this room, move on to the next.

Declutter your space by throwing away, recycling, or donating anything you do not need or use. Dedicate decorative boxes, containers, or baskets for specific items. Rearrange furniture to create more open space.

Technique #2

Divide and conquer a clean house by delegating those in your household or other volunteers willing to help. These volunteers may be friends, family, or neighbors, or they may be from local groups or organizations. Delegate one room per person or tackle one room at a time as a team.

Technique #3

If able, hire a cleaning service to organize and clean your space for you.

STRATEGY #2

DAILY SCHEDULE

Create a Daily Schedule for each day of the week. This is the routine you will follow every day.

Include things such as your morning wake-up and bedtime, meal time, medication time, personal time, and anything else you usually do throughout your day.

Write it on a piece of paper, draw it in table form, or create a template on the computer.

Place this schedule in a place you will undoubtedly see every day, such as your refrigerator, kitchen table, or posted on the bathroom mirror.

Technique #1

- 6:00 a.m. WAKE UP
- 6:15 a.m. Morning Journal, Meditation, Self Check-In
- 6:30 a.m. *My* breakfast
- 7:00 a.m. Shower
- 7:30 a.m. Wash and change [loved one]
- 8:00 a.m. Feed [loved one] breakfast
- 8:30 a.m. Give medicines to [loved one]

…and so on through bedtime.

STRATEGY #3

CALENDAR or PLANNER

Mark appointments on a Calendar or a Planner.

This will help you keep track of things such as the next doctor or healthcare appointment, a date with your spouse or a friend, or special occasions you'd like to remember, like birthdays or parties.

Strategy #4

LOGS or RECORDS

Keep a Log or Record for things such as medications, toileting, bathing, repositioning, feeding, and visitors.

For example, when giving medications frequently, it can be hard to remember what time you gave the last dose, how much you gave, and when you can give the next dose.

Keep a written record of the medication you gave, what time you gave it, how much (the dose) you gave, and whether it was effective.

Technique #1

Monday

- Morphine 0.5 ml @ 8:00 a.m. – **Helped Pain**
- Morphine 0.5 ml @ 12:00 p.m. – **Helped Pain**
- Lorazepam 0.25ml @ 12:00 p.m. – **Helped Anxiety**

See my FREE giveaway,
The Crucial Toolkit For End-Of-Life Care
at the end of this book to request a sample medication log.

Strategy #5

ALARMS & REMINDERS

Set Alarms and Reminders on your phone.

Set these alarms for important things you do not want to forget, especially if the task is in the near future.

For example,

- Set an alarm to give your loved one's next dose of medication.
- Set an alarm to wake up after a 20-minute nap.
- Set an alarm to remind yourself to step outside the house at sunset.

STRATEGY #6

TO-DO LISTS & CHECKLISTS

Keep To-Do lists and Checklists for anything you can think of.

This might include groceries, phone calls to make, emails to write, and errands to run.

Prioritize essential tasks that need to get done today and draw a line through them when completed. Crossing things off your list will feel so good. Then slowly work through the rest.

Helpful Hint

Delegate tasks to others whenever possible.

TIP #2
CATCHIN' Z's

"Sleep is all about recovering. So if you're not sleeping, you're not recovering. And if you're going to break your body down a lot, you better find ways to build it back up. And the only way to do that is get a lot of sleep."

- Tom Brady

I'M NOT USUALLY one to get sick often, but when I do, it's because I've been running around and barely sleeping. I learned this lesson while working as a hospice nurse in my mid-twenties. It was wintertime. We were amid a busy season, as most holiday seasons go. A little short-staffed at the time, I had volunteered to work on-call at night in addition to my typical day shifts. It felt important and necessary that I step up being the young, healthy, and vibrant twenty-something-year-old that I was. Plus, our patients and families needed someone, and I wanted to be there for them.

I was probably about a week in when I started to feel my body failing, but I shook it off like it was nothing. However, by the end of week two, I was constantly lightheaded, exhausted, and, quite honestly, just didn't look right.

I drove home for Christmas to be with my family. It was only supposed to be for a few days. I needed to get back to my patients and their families. Christmas morning, I stood up to hug my Dad, and the next thing I knew, I woke up on the floor, my Dad flustered and scared, not knowing what had just happened. I had fainted, and it freaked us both out.

I spent the entire day lying on a hospital bed in the Emergency Room that Christmas Day. A ton of blood work, IVs, and several hours later, my discharge instructions were clear: sleep and rest.

So much for going back to work. I ended up being down for the count for over a week. We went from short-staffed to shorter-staffed, all because I didn't give my body the sleep and rest it needed.

Lesson learned.

When you're tired, can you function at your best? While many of us believe we operate "just fine" on little sleep, the science says otherwise. Sleep is a fundamental part of our health. Not only does sleep help our body and mind reset and recharge, but research shows that a lack of sleep can have several negative health effects. These include mood fluctuations, risk of depression, an inability to concentrate, and we're more likely to make mistakes. It also increases the risk of disease in general.

According to experts, adults between the ages of 18-61 need at least seven hours of sleep each night, while adults aged 65 and up need seven-to-eight hours. To improve the quality of your sleep and sleep pattern, incorporate these simple tricks.

STRATEGY #1

Go to bed and wake up at the *same* time every day, making sure to give yourself at least seven hours of sleep each night.

STRATEGY #2

Close all window shades and curtains to keep your bedroom dark.

STRATEGY #3

Shut the bedroom door to block out noise. A noise machine or bedside fan may add additional white noise.

STRATEGY #4

Stop using electronic devices, such as cell phones, televisions, or computers, at least 30 minutes before bed. They stimulate the brain and prevent us from falling asleep.

STRATEGY #5

Avoid caffeine, alcohol, or big meals near bedtime.

STRATEGY #6

Meditate before bed.

Strategy #7

Listen to your body. Even if you've had enough sleep at night, sometimes you may need an extra nap during the day to rejuvenate.

After you've had a chance to feed, toilet, change, and get your loved one settled in their bed or in a chair watching television, allow yourself to lie down and doze off for a 20-minute nap.
Do this once in the morning and maybe even once in the afternoon if needed.

If you are concerned about their safety, think about using a bed or chair alarm that will wake you if they try to move on their own.

TIP #3
GOOD M-OOOR-NING!

"But, there is still every reason for healthy people to take cold showers or swim outside in cold water. It gives you the feeling that you are alive."

- Wim Hof

ARE you waking up feeling exhausted, fatigued, or just not ready to start the day? First thing in the morning, hop in the shower to help your body and mind wake up. For the last ten seconds or more, turn the shower knob on cold to jumpstart your mind and body.

There are many times in my life when I routinely get up at 5:00 a.m., and nothing, I mean *nothing,* wakes me up like the jolt of cold water hitting my skin. When I started taking cold morning showers, oh man, was it rough. I'd scream in the shower, *"OKAY, OKAY, I'm awake! That's enough!"* While I didn't look forward to it, I always felt amazing afterward. So, every morning I kept turning that knob. To this day, cold showers still give me a pep in my step, but I can now report they are something I also enjoy.

Cold showers aren't always easy to get used to. Still, research shows they not only help you wake up but can also boost your immune system, decrease pain, and help your body recover faster.

TIP #4
WASH IT OFF

"I shower in the dark, barely able to tell soap from conditioner, and tell myself that I will emerge new and strong, that the water will heal me."

- Veronica Roth

HAVE you ever taken a hot shower after a long, hard, draining day? What does it feel like? Every evening, take another shower to help you *unload* your day by rinsing it all off. This time, allow yourself a nice, hot, soothing shower or bath to help your body and mind relax.The warmth of the water rushing over you feels like it's washing all your stress away.

Research suggests that bathing has several benefits, whether in a shower, bath, or at the sink. It washes toxins off our bodies and boosts our immune system. More surprisingly, it also has "feel-good" effects, which help to relieve stress, increase happiness, and improve sleep.

Helpful Hint

Try adding bath salts, bath bombs, or essential oils such as lavender for added relaxation.

Tip #5
'Tooth' Be Told

"Self-care is your fuel ... Whatever the road ahead or the path you've taken, self-care is what keeps your motor running and your wheels turning."

- Melissa Steginus

BRUSH YOUR TEETH, preferably with fluoride toothpaste, every morning and every night. Floss at least once a day.

Sounds simple, right?

How many times have you woken up late and had to run out the door, realizing I'd be covering up my overnight breath with coffee? And how many times have you passed out on the couch just to wake up at 2:00 a.m. with the television still on, dragging yourself up to bed, blindly thinking, "I should really brush my teeth…" and not? I'll admit, I've been guilty of both.

When we're already late or just totally exhausted, mouth care is one of those things that is easily forgotten or intentionally left out. But we all know the feeling of a freshly cleaned mouth. Not only does it make us *feel* good and refreshed (It really does, doesn't it?), but it's also one of the best ways to prevent infections. So, brush up!

TIP #6

CLEAN CLOTHES, FRESH START

"Nobody can go back and start a new beginning, but anyone can start today and make a new ending."

- Maria Robinson

FOR SEVERAL YEARS, I worked with an older gentleman named Joe, a full-time caregiver for his wife. Joe's wife had several chronic illnesses for which she had required more and more of his help over the last twelve years. There was something about Joe that inspired me. Joe always seemed so happy. Every visit, rain or shine, good day or bad. He was always friendly, smiling, and cheerful. So as I got to know Joe and his wife, I had to ask for his secret. It was his wife who, usually quiet and meek, chuckled and burst out, "It's his clothes!"

I thought it was pretty funny myself until I heard his reasoning. I came to find out that for as long as they had known each other, every night before bed, Joe would lay out clean clothes for the next day. He said it was his reminder: "Every day is a new day. Clean and fresh like the clothes on my back."

———

When you aren't often leaving the house, it's easy to get into the habit of wearing old, comfy clothes such as sweatpants and cozy T-shirts. While I support putting on lounge clothes some days, there is something to be said about putting on clothes that make you *feel* refreshed. So do your best to put on clean clothes every morning.

Choose clothes that, when you look in the mirror, you think to yourself, "Okay, I can do this." Even if yesterday was a rough day, like the clean clothes on your back, today brings a fresh start, new opportunities, and a clean template. As silly as it sounds, clothes that make you feel good can boost your self-confidence and self-esteem at the start of your day. Even on your worst days, they can make you feel like you will make it and you will be okay.

STRATEGY #1

Lay your clothes out before going to bed so you won't have to think about it when you first wake up in the morning while in a sleepy stupor.

TIP #7
FRESH NAILS

"Take care of your body. It's the only place you have to live."

- Jim Rohn

I KNOW what you're thinking. You're thinking, "Seriously? Why is this a necessary tip?" Think about it...

As your loved one's caregiver, you'll likely be helping them wash, toilet, and dress. So naturally, you can expect to come in contact with their urine, feces, and possibly vomit. Unfortunately, these sneaky little germs like to find their way under your nails for safe keeping and eventually find your eyeballs. Oh, great. Just what you needed – pink eye. To help prevent bugs and bacteria from spreading unnecessarily, wash your hands several times a day while paying particular attention to under your nails.

STRATEGY #1

Wash your hands with soap and water before and after providing personal care for your loved one. Using a small scrub brush, focus on cleaning underneath your nails.

STRATEGY #2

Consider wearing gloves, especially anytime their urine, stool, or vomit are involved.

STRATEGY #3

Keep your nails trimmed as needed.

TIP #8

EAT FOOD

"Your body is your machine - you need your fuel."

- Cassie Scerbo

THE TERM 'HANGRY' is "a state of anger caused by a lack of food; hunger causing a negative change in emotional state." I don't know about you, but I've definitely had my share of 'hangry' moments. I apologize to all those who've been on the other end of my 'hanger.'

For some people, eating in the morning has always been unappealing. Add the turmoil of emotion tag along with caregiving, and you may lose your appeal for food altogether. But, please trust me when I say food is your teammate in this caregiving venture. Food is not only life-sustaining but essential to maintaining our caregiving abilities. So, even if it's small, eat breakfast, lunch, and dinner. Just get something in you.

Your caregiving days often start with a *bang*, and before you know it, it's evening, and you haven't eaten a single thing all day. Starting your day with a little fuel can go a long way. After a long night of fasting (not eating), food gives your body the nutrients it needs to provide you with a boost in energy, mood, concentration, and alertness. In addition, some research shows that eating breakfast might decrease the risk of disease. So, make sure you are feeding and fueling yourself. Your body and mind won't run on fumes forever, and your loved one is counting on you to be at your best.

Choose food options that nourish your body, mind, and soul. Foods such as fresh fruits, vegetables, lean proteins, healthy fats (nuts, seeds, fish, olive oil), and whole grains give you the steady energy and balanced stamina you need to get you through your day. While sugar and caffeine give you quick bursts of energy, a fast crash soon follows. Do your best to stick with what keeps your energy level stable.

Saying that, we're all human! There will undoubtedly be times you prefer to soothe your emotions by eating foods that bring you comfort, and that's perfectly valid. I encourage you to recognize how different foods make you *feel* both physically and mentally. Then, stick with those that keep you feeling positive and energized.

Quick, inexpensive, and easy breakfast options include a bowl of oatmeal or whole grain cereal. Add fresh fruit like strawberries or blueberries for flavor. Cook eggs in various ways. Top yogurt with seeds, nuts, or fresh fruit. Or spread peanut butter on a banana.

Provide your body with the nourishment it needs to keep you going. If you are like me and breakfast has never been your thing, or you just don't have an appetite, here are three easy ways to ensure you get the nourishment you need.

STRATEGY #1

Every time you feed your loved one, feed yourself, too. Give them one bite, then give yourself one bite. Continue until you are both done with your meal.

STRATEGY #2

Create your own meal schedule. Designate specific times to feed your-self three to five times per day.

For example….

- Dedicate 7:00-7:30 a.m. *as your* breakfast time.
- Dedicate 12:00-12:30 p.m. as *your* lunchtime.
- Dedicate 6:30-7:30 p.m. as *your* dinner time.

STRATEGY #3

On Sundays (or whatever day of the week you choose), create a meal plan for your week ahead and add it to your schedule. When you have your meals planned ahead of time and maybe even pre-prepared, you won't have to *think* you can simply *do*.

TIP #9
DRINK, DRINK, DRINK... WATER

"Do something today that your future self will thank you for."

- Sean Patrick Flanery

BORING, right? – drinking water.

Dehydration is one of those things that can sneak up on you out of the blue. Our bodies usually do a good job keeping us hydrated by sparking our thirst. Still, it's a lot easier to get dehydrated than most of us think.

While working in the hospital, I was constantly on my feet, running from room to room, caring for my patients. Sure, there were times I'd be thirsty, which was my body reminding me to sneak a sip from my water bottle, but one day I ignored the urge. I was too busy to stop, so I didn't. Eventually, my thirst disappeared, but by the end of the day, my head was pounding. I felt lightheaded, dizzy and even a little nauseous, dehydration setting in. Thankfully, I was off of work the following day, the sensations only worsening overnight. However, it took several days of little activity and consistent water intake to get myself feeling right again.

Got it - Water - *Check*.

Keeping your body hydrated is critical for many reasons. The right water balance in your body can help to maintain your body temperature, decrease the risk of infection, keep your joints mobile, carry crucial nutrients to the cells in your body, and support the function of your organs.

Unless you have specific healthcare practitioner recommendations, research says women should drink approximately 11 cups of water per day. In comparison, men should drink approximately 16 cups per day. However, be aware it is possible and dangerous to be 'over-hydrated,' so always discuss the best amount with your provider.

Try to limit liquids loaded with sugar or artificial sweeteners such as soda pop, fruit juices, and energy and electrolyte drinks. While this can be tough, you don't have to stick with drinking plain water. To those of you who either find it hard or get bored of drinking plain water, I can relate. I often alternate several different tactics to trick myself into staying hydrated. You can, too.

STRATEGY #1

Use visual cues. Keep a filled cup, glass, or water bottle next to you throughout the day. When sitting right in front of you, you're more likely to take occasional sips.

STRATEGY #2

Set an alarm to remind yourself to keep drinking throughout the day. Every time your alarm goes off, take a few small sips.

STRATEGY #3

Squeeze lemon, lime, or add a few mint leaves to your glass.

STRATEGY #4

You can also flavor your water by infusing it with fruits or vegetables such as berries, orange slices, or cucumber slices.

STRATEGY #5

Sparkling water, coffee, and tea can are other adequate liquids to help keep you hydrated and offer a change of pace to water.

Tip #10
"When You Gotta Go... Go!"

"If I want to be alone, some place I can write, I can read, I can pray, I can cry, I can do whatever I want - I go to the bathroom."

- Alicia Keys

USE THE BATHROOM/TOILET whenever you feel the urge. I know it sounds silly, but it's the truth. I know what it's like to work 12-going-on-25-hours a day, constantly caring for others, and barely having a moment's rest to empty my bladder. Fortunately, I was lucky to learn this tip from colleagues who wound up with infections or worse.

Holding your urine too long increases the risk of urinary tract infections and kidney injuries. It can also weaken your bladder muscles which can cause you to leak urine unintentionally. This is known as incontinence.

Holding your bowel movements for too long can lead to problems such as constipation and bowel blockage. A blockage of stool in the colon or rectum is known as an impaction. When an impaction develops, the bowels cannot move. It may require a combination of medications and manual procedures to unblock. So, rule of thumb – "When you gotta go, *go!*"

Helpful Hint

Strengthen your pelvic floor muscles (AKA your pee and poo muscles) by practicing Kegel exercises. Do this by tightening your bathroom muscles - the same muscles you would use to hold in your pee - for five to ten seconds at a time. Continue doing this five to ten times in a row – holding, releasing, holding, releasing.

TIP #11
EXERCISE

"If you are in a bad mood go for a walk. If you are still in a bad mood go for another walk."

- Hippocrates

WHEN MY GRANDDAD WAS DYING, I was working two jobs and traveling over an hour each way to help care for him. At the same time, being the nurse practitioner in the family, I felt responsible for preparing my family for his dying process while supporting them mentally and emotionally. Sure I was constantly *moving*, but it wasn't movement that could help me release the tension that was building inside me.

For most of my life, I've been a sucker for a good kick-in-the-butt workout that would allow me to "sweat it all out," but I hadn't had the time to get my fill. I'd been at this routine for weeks when there finally came a day when my usual patience was wearing thin. I was irritable and snappy and then, of course, felt guilty about it. My body was tense, so my mind and spirit were simply following suit.

One evening, as tired as I was, I decided to go for a walk. That short walk felt so good. It was the reminder I needed to get back to my detox, which for me meant a sweaty workout. It didn't matter how tired I was, I knew I had to make exercise a priority, and so I did. Despite waking up even earlier, I found I had *more* energy to give to all those around me.

Worth it.

Move your body. This means doing some form of exercise.

> "But I'm already moving all day long taking care of my loved one. I'm exhausted. I don't have the energy to do anything else. And now, you're telling me to exercise...?!"

Yes. This is exactly what I am saying. So hang in there with me as I explain the benefits. As tired as you are, a little exercise can keep your body, mind, and spirit *stronger, healthier, and happier.* Research shows physical activity improves your mood, increases your concentration, helps you sleep better at night, and is an incredible stress reliever. Exercise links directly and indirectly to improved self-esteem, self-image, and self-confidence.

While the daily recommendation is to incorporate 150 minutes of exercise per week, you're probably already doing most of it without even knowing! Activities such as vacuuming, gardening, taking out the trash, and walking the dog count toward those total minutes. Five minutes here, ten minutes there, doing little bits of movement for short bursts throughout the day will add up before you know it.

Other forms of exercise such as biking, running, swimming, hiking, weight-lifting, or even doing push-ups require a bit more *intensity* but will boost your heart rate and improve your overall health and well-being. These are the types of activities I use to help me release any built-up tension.

Again, I know there will be days when you just don't have the energy for these higher-intensity activities. And that's okay. When you don't have it in you, do something fun that brings a smile to your face, such as dancing, tossing a ball, or playing games in the park. Yoga, Tai Chi, Pilates, or simply stretching are other forms of exercise that can be rejuvenating. They can improve your mood, flexibility, strength, balance, and well-being.

Try your best. 30 minutes a day, five days a week. *Move* your body. I know for many of you, exercise will *not* be easy right now. So if you miss a day, don't get down on yourself. If you run out of time today, make yourself a promise to do a little movement tomorrow. Remember, a little movement can go a long way. Start small, then slowly look to improve.

You got this, my friend.
Yes, you can. Yes, you will.

Your body deserves this, and so do your mind and spirit.

TIP #12
YOUR HEALTH & MEDICAL CARE

"To keep the body in good health is a duty... otherwise we shall not be able to keep our mind strong and clear."

- Buddha

I WORKED with a daughter named Mel, the primary and full-time caregiver for her elderly mother. Mel's mother couldn't do anything for herself, requiring Mel to be with her most of every day. Mel was thoroughly exhausted and burning out fast. She also had health problems of her own, which she often put on the back burner. Mel missed her healthcare appointments and never had time to refill her medications. She had other family members, but none offered help or care relief.

I was scheduled for a visit later that day when I got the call. Mel had a bad fall earlier that morning. Her mother was somehow able to get to the phone to call 911. At the hospital, doctors told Mel she had suffered a heart attack. She would be unable to care for her mother and, instead, would need care of her own. This tip came as a result.

Take care of your medical and health conditions. While I expect your current concern is primarily your loved one's condition and overall comfort level, it's crucial to stay on top of your health, too.

Why?

Because you must stay healthy to continue caring for them, they're relying on you. Some of you may be living with chronic diseases or disorders such as heart problems, high blood pressure, diabetes or blood sugar problems, lung disease like asthma or COPD, kidney problems, arthritis or painful joints, osteoporosis or weak bones, or others. You might also be someone with no health problems at all. Either way, use these strategies to stay well and continue giving your loved one your best.

STRATEGY #1

HEALTHCARE APPOINTMENTS

Make sure you are scheduling and keeping your healthcare appointments. Whether going for an annual well-visit, check-up, or specialist visit, continue following up on your health status. No matter your current health status, you've got to keep yourself in check.

STRATEGY #2

SHARE YOUR CONCERNS

Be sure to tell your healthcare practitioner you are a caregiver. Share with your healthcare practitioner how you feel mentally, emotionally, and physically.

For example, communicate with your practitioner if you are feeling down, depressed, or hopeless. They can help you find support, resources, and guidance to cope. Depending on you and your practitioner, medications such as antidepressants may be appropriate to help you through this difficult time.

Additionally, be sure to tell them if you are feeling sick in any way.

STRATEGY #3

MEDICATION MANAGEMENT

If you take medicine to manage your blood pressure, blood sugar, or other health problem, continue taking them as directed by your healthcare practitioner. With your day-to-day caregiving needs, you often lose track of time, making it easy to forget these things. Use these techniques such as the following to help you.

Technique #1

Set alarms to remind you to take your medication, check your blood pressure, or check your blood sugar at the appropriate time.

Technique #2

Use a medicine planner. This container helps you organize your medicine by both day and time.

Choose a day of the week to fill your medications in your medicine planner routinely. Pre-filling your medicine planner will help remind you to take your medications the following week.

Always double- or triple-check that your planner is filled correctly and exactly as your healthcare practitioner prescribes.

Technique #3

Keep a log that specifies when you took your medication, checked your blood pressure, or checked your blood sugar.

Also, track your blood pressure and blood sugar numbers each day.

TIP #13
PRACTICE ACCEPTANCE

"Grant me the serenity to accept the things I cannot change, the courage to change the things I can and the wisdom to know the difference."

- Reinhold Niebuhr

IT IS in the moments that most challenge us, in the times that seem most unfair, and in the situations that appear to be our greatest obstacles that trigger us to resist hardship. We begin to lose faith in ourselves, our life, and the Universe (or whatever higher power you may or may not believe in). We begin to question everything. Caregiving is one of those challenging, sometimes unfair, obstacles we face. We think…

"Why me?"
"Why them?"
"Why now?"
"How could this happen?"

"How could _____ let this happen?"

The truth is, there are no answers to these questions. They are ambiguous and, in actuality, won't and don't make you *feel* any better. Neither does finding someone to blame. Answers or not, blame or not, your loved one still needs care. This cannot be changed. Yet we often waste enormous mental, emotional, and spiritual energy on finding answers, needing to know, and continuing to point blame. This only contributes to negativity filling your soul.

Dear Caregiver,
This important tip is to remind you there is simply no reason to spend your energy wondering about things no one can change. You can trust me because I've been there.

Free yourself from the weight, stress, and negative energy you are holding onto by giving yourself permission to let go of the unanswer-able. You will feel *lighter.* There is peace in accepting what you cannot change. There is serenity in accepting what you cannot control. Accep-tance is a higher power. And it is a gift to your mental health. When you practice acceptance, you embrace grace.

STRATEGY #1

Every morning...

- Practice accepting your current situation.
- Practice accepting your loved one's disease, illness, diagnosis, or prognosis for what it is.
- Practice accepting and acknowledging their time here with you is not infinite.

No matter your feelings about it, accept the reality. By doing so, you will begin to restore wholeness.

TIP #14
HONOR YOUR CHOICE

"No matter what the situation, remind yourself, you have a choice."

- Deepak Chopra

WHILE IT MAY FEEL like you had no choice but to care for your loved one, the truth is, you did. You always had a choice. And you always have a choice. Even if your loved one had no one else to care for them, you decided to be the one to take on this important role. Everything we do in life is a choice. This is no exception.

Regardless of how you feel about being their caregiver in this given moment, take a minute or two every day to honor yourself for choosing your caregiver role. When going through these strategies, focus on the positives. Revisit these reflections often.

STRATEGY #1

Spend some time reflecting on why you decided to take on this challenging yet gratifying role.

For example…

Maybe you are a child caring for your parent, a grandchild caring for your grandparent, or a niece or nephew caring for your aunt or uncle.

- Are you giving back what they gave to you when you were young?

- Or are you giving them what they could not give you when you were young?

Maybe you are someone attempting to set an example for others to look up to.

- Are you a parent setting an example for a child?
- Are you a daughter or son setting an example for another sibling?
- Are you a friend setting an example for your community?

Maybe you feel this role falls in line with your morals and values.

By embodying the duty of a caregiver, you are aligning yourself with compassion, civility, and grace, just to name a few. When times are tough, reconnect to these genuine, admirable, and deeply inspiring motives.

STRATEGY #2

Ask yourself these questions:

- What opportunity does caring for my loved one offer me that I otherwise would not have?
- How does the experience of providing end-of-life care for my loved one make me a stronger person?
- How does caring for my loved one strengthen my relationships? With my loved one? With others?
- How is caring for my loved one rewarding?
- What gift am I experiencing by caring for my loved one?

STRATEGY #3

Remind yourself that you are never stuck. Sometimes when we make big, important decisions, such as this one, we suddenly feel trapped with no way out.

The reality is *time* gives us *new* information. Time and new information can give us different perspectives we may not have seen or known before.

It's okay to realize that although you chose to be your loved one's caregiver, you now must continue to honor yourself by making a different choice. Just because you made this choice doesn't mean it will be the right choice forever.

The worst thing you can do is move forward with your caregiving choice when it no longer feels right. You don't want anyone to feel hurt. You don't want to look "bad." You don't want to deal with the aftermath. But that doesn't mean you continue to take on a caregiving role you no longer align with.

It's not about being unloving or unaccountable. It's about honoring yourself.

You have permission to change your mind.

TIP #15
STEER CLEAR OF PERFECTION

"A beautiful thing is never perfect."

- Egyptian proverb

SO MANY OF us strive for "perfection." The need for perfection typically stems from childhood. It often develops as a learned response after making a mistake. As children, we learn that mistakes are bad, and out of this comes a belief that to be good, loved, and accepted, we must also be perfect.

But perfection is not the key, you see. Perfection isn't real. It does not exist. It's an illusion. Making mistakes is part of being human. Rather than seek out perfection, search for ways to improve. *That* is the secret.

This is also true when it comes to caregiving. It's easy and all too common to blame ourselves when something "bad" happens. You blame yourself for their pain or discomfort. You feel guilty whenever you need to undress them or change their soiled diapers. You fault yourself for giving their medicine late or forgetting altogether. Or maybe you even feel responsible for their eventual death. The guilt you take on can be unbearable.

Dear Caregiver,

My friend, you must stop. Stop blaming yourself. Stop holding on to that guilt. There is no such thing as a "perfect" caregiver. And you are *no* exception. So, please, go easy on yourself. It takes courage to get back up after you've made a mistake. But, keep going. Keep learning. A beautiful part of the human experience is our growth.

Practice these strategies to help yourself let go of always trying to be "perfect."

STRATEGY #1

USE EMPOWERING AFFIRMATIONS

Write them down. Repeat them to yourself. Feel them deeply.

To get yourself started, here are some examples:

- "I am proud of myself for learning and evolving."
- "It's okay not to get it right all the time. I am doing the best I can with what I know right now."
- "I am committing to things that nourish my soul while also honoring my boundaries when things feel overly exhausting."
- "I am allowing myself to grow by choosing to let go of my mistakes."
- "I trust myself and have faith in the decisions I make."
- "I am freeing myself of guilt as it no longer serves me."
- "I am enough."

- "I am choosing to forgive myself. I am allowing my
  mistakes to be opportunities to learn from."

Believe it. Believe in *you.*

Focus on what you *can* do. Focus on all the selfless and amazing things
you *are* doing. Focus on the *care* you are providing.

You are doing your best, and that is all that matters. Truly.

TIP #16
SELF CHECK-IN

"Our bodies communicate to us clearly and specifically, if we are willing to listen to them."

- Shakti Gawain

ONCE A DAY OR ONCE A WEEK, practice what I like to call a "self check-in." This means being honest with yourself and how you're *really* doing.

How are you feeling mentally, physically, emotionally, spiritually, socially, environmentally, financially, and occupationally?

While we mentioned these aspects of wellness earlier, it's necessary to work through each of the eight parts that make up your overall well-being. Ask yourself questions. Be honest with your answers. Dig deep and allow yourself to be wherever you are, good or bad. The strategies below are examples of how you might start to work through the different dimensions that make up your whole.

Strategy #1

CHECK-IN WITH YOUR MIND

Having been in your shoes, I'll take a guess and say that all you do is think about your loved one morning, noon, and night. Your mind can't seem to stop worrying or stressing about them. It's nonstop.

As a result, **Dear Caregiver**, you aren't allowing yourself to feel. You are not giving yourself the space to acknowledge or process any of your own emotions. Instead, you may be lashing out at others or bottling everything inside.

When dealing with difficult or painful emotions, most of us learn to cope by ignoring, diminishing, or pretending they do not exist. And as a result, you now react in one of those two ways: blowing up or bottling.

The problem is that these difficult emotions *do* exist. They won't just "go away" by dismissing them. In fact, research shows that doing so can lead to anxiety, depression, sickness, substance abuse, and even suicide. So, it's time to check in with yourself.

Technique #1

JOURNALING

Every day, spend anywhere from 60 seconds to 20 minutes checking in with yourself through journaling.

I know, I know. Some of you will now be saying, "I don't journal," or "Journaling is a waste of my time," or "I don't have time to journal," or "What will journaling do for me?"

Stay with me here…

Research shows journaling has numerous benefits. It can help reduce stress, anxiety, and depression. It also allows you to organize your thoughts, bringing clarity and peace of mind. Journaling can help open your mind to new solutions. Finally, it can boost your immune system, improve sleep, and strengthen your connection to your body, mind, and soul.

While no one journal needs to look the same, here are five daily journal prompts to try out…

- What seems to be [the thing] bothering me most today? (A concern, a worry, a stressor, a person)
- How is this [above thing] making me feel? Pick one emotion that best fits. (Identify and name the emotion. Example: Sad, Angry, Fearful)
- Why is this [above thing] making me feel [emotion above]?
- What is one thing I can do today to improve the [above thing]?
- I am grateful for [above thing] because… (Is it teaching you something? Is it helping you grow in some way? Is there a lesson to learn from? Is it giving you an opportunity in some way?)
- I will make today a better day by _____.
- Today, I am… [acknowledge something positive about myself] (Example: Today, I am doing my best.)

Taking your jumbled thoughts to paper helps you acknowledge feelings you may have been ignoring, hiding, or refusing to accept. As you write, don't be surprised if you become aware of emotions you didn't know existed. Journaling is a simple and easy way to release those things you've been tucking away for a later date.
It allows you to safely "let everything out" so you aren't bottling it all up…

So that they don't continue to build inside you...
So that you won't suddenly implode...
So that you won't reach your breaking point...

I know journaling isn't always an easy habit to pick up. So keep it simple. Keep your journal and pen (or paper and pencil) next to your bed, or somewhere you will be forced to see it every day. You'll remember to open it up and write when you see it. Whether it is 60 seconds or whether it is 20 minutes, don't miss it. You will begin to find mental clarity and ease as you set your feelings free.

STRATEGY #2

CHECK-IN WITH YOUR BODY

Similarly, try checking in with your body.

When stressed, overwhelmed, tired, or holding onto certain emotions, we often carry tension in different areas of our bodies. Again, spend anywhere from 60 seconds to five minutes (or more) noticing and acknowledging the sensations within your body. While you can do this with a journal, I have found mindfulness and meditation practices keep me grounded. You know you best, so use whatever works best for you, and don't be afraid to try something new.

For guidance, here are four quick body check-in questions to journal, meditate on, or be mindful of...

- How does my body feel today? (Do a quick scan from head to toe.)
- Where in my body do I feel the most tension?
- What can I do to help relieve this tension even slightly?
- On a scale of one to ten, how much energy does my body have today?

- (one being the least, ten being the most)
- What number on this scale means my body needs more rest?
- What can I do to make my body feel good or better today?

Allow your body to be your guide...

If your body needs rest, pause.

If your body needs movement, move.

If your body needs exercise, workout.

If your body needs sleep, close your eyes and lie down.

If your body needs food, eat.

If your body needs comfort, give it comfort, whether that be a hot shower, a bath, a hug, or a warm mug of hot chocolate next to a fire.

If your body needs love, hug yourself, hug your loved one, or hug anyone willing nearby.

TIP #17
BE THE STUDENT

"The important thing is not to stop questioning. Curiosity has its own reason for existence. One cannot help but be in awe when he contemplates the mysteries of eternity, of life, of the marvelous structure of reality. It is enough if one tries merely to comprehend a little of this mystery each day.

- Albert Einstein

WHEN MY FRIEND, Kyle, was given a whopping cancer diagnosis, it scared us all. We struggled to wrap our brains around this news.

What *did* it mean? How bad was it? Was it curable? Would it spread? Has it already spread? What would *that* mean? Were there treatment options? Was time with my friend limited?

None of us knew what to expect. None of us knew what to do. But being the instinctual student I am, always needing to know what I don't know, I began researching. I found out all that I could about Kyle's new cancer diagnosis. I looked up everything from his type of cancer to how it might affect him, average life expectancy to reliable treatment options, and the costs, benefits, and risks of each. I looked up "how to help a friend with cancer" and "how to start a fundraiser."

I shared everything I learned with Kyle and his family. Somehow, having this information gave us all some comfort. Was it still scary? It sure was. But at least it wasn't so unknown anymore. Having some knowledge gave Kyle, his family, and myself a way to plan and prepare for what was to come.

––––––––––

Families are often surprised and unprepared to care for a loved one, reporting the lack of understanding around their loved one's "prognosis." The prognosis is how the healthcare provider expects your loved one's disease, sickness, or illness to evolve or progress over time. Additionally, family caregivers are unaware of resources and other services available to assist them or the extent of physical and personal care their loved ones will require.

Research shows this lack of preparedness and education increases healthcare costs and overall health risks for families, especially family caregivers. These health risks include complicated and long-term grief, mood fluctuations such as depression and anxiety, sleep problems, and a poorer quality of life. Your healthcare team should hopefully provide the tools, guidance, and support needed to feel informed and ready to care for your loved one. However, always seek to learn anything you don't know.

An informed caregiver is a prepared caregiver. And being prepared will help you cope in times of stress, overwhelm, and even sadness. It will help you be the best caregiver you can be. Like most things in life, you feel less anxious when you know what to expect in any given situation. Because let's face it, we don't like *unknowns*.

The same theory applies here. When you know what to expect as your loved one's disease progresses – for instance, what they might go through or experience, how they will change, and how you can help them – you won't feel like you're in the dark. You won't feel as anxious. You won't feel as afraid. You *will* feel more confident in your ability to control the situation and, in the process, feel less overwhelmed by it. So learn!

Learn as much as you can…

- About what you can expect next, and then again after that.
- About what you need to know as a caregiver.
- About medications you may have to give your loved one.
- About equipment you may have to help your loved one use.
- About resources, benefits, and the services available to you.
- About how to take care of yourself in this entire process.

When the time comes, learn about the dying process. My guidebook, *The Dying Process: Understanding Signs, Symptoms & Changes At The End-Of-Life,* is a resource to help with just that.

Learn about everything and anything. There are books, online tools, local classes, and more to help you understand what your loved one is going through and the many ways you can help care for them. Be sure to ask your healthcare team about resources and information they can provide you. Self-education is the path to self-confidence.

TIP #18
ASK QUESTIONS

"He who asks a question is a fool for five minutes; he who does not ask a question remains a fool forever."

- Chinese Proverb

IT IS *ALWAYS* good to ask your healthcare or hospice team any questions you might have. I always tell my patients and their families, "No question is a stupid question!" As well as, "You are allowed to repeat the same question as many times as you need!" I love when families ask me questions because it helps me judge how clear I am being and what might need more explanation.

Caring for a loved one is hard, making words and information difficult to digest, especially if it happens near the loved one's end of life. Feel encouraged to repeat the same question over and over. You're going through so much right now. No one expects you to remember everything that is said to you.

If you're thinking, "I don't know what questions to even ask," here are questions you might ask your healthcare or hospice team:

- What types of signs, symptoms, and changes will my loved one experience?
- What can I do to help and support my loved one best?
- What am I expected to do for my loved one now that they are home?
- What medications (and how much of each) should my loved one take- if any?
- Based on what you've experienced, how do you think my loved one's disease will progress and how quickly?
- What resources are available to help me care for my loved one?
- What equipment will my loved one need, and how do I use them all?
- What should I do if my loved one is having an emergency or if we have urgent questions?

Remember, if you don't ask, your healthcare team won't know what you don't know.

Helpful Hint

Download my FREE resource *The Crucial Toolkit For End-Of-Life Care* found at the end of this book for additional questions.

TIP #19
BE THE PARROT

"To effectively communicate, we must realize that we are all different in the way we perceive the world and use this understanding as a guide to our communication with others."

- Tony Robbins

ROB WAS NEWLY DIAGNOSED with Diabetes. As his nurse practitioner, I saw him at home to help him understand and adjust to this new disease. On top of the emotional jolt of the news, Rob was attempting to digest a lot of new information. He was overwhelmed. It meant a total lifestyle change from here on out, and I wanted to be sure he felt comfortable with it.

After several visits, it became clear that we weren't on the same page. Either I wasn't being clear enough, or he didn't understand me, or both. So we came up with a deal that he would reiterate everything he understood from our time together before I left each visit. He became a parrot. Because of this, we developed a stronger rapport and a more confident relationship.

Constant communication is key.

Whether you think you have missed something or not, it's always a good idea to recap what you've heard and understood to your healthcare team. We all have different ways of thinking, digesting, and communicating information. The simple act of reiteration will confirm your interpretation and free you from second-guessing yourself in the future. Here are easy ways to talk to your healthcare and hospice team.

STRATEGY #1

Directly communicate with your healthcare professional your desire to echo what you've heard them say.

- I'd like to repeat what I have just heard you say to make sure I didn't miss anything.
- I will reiterate what you just said to ensure my understanding is correct.

It takes open and consistent communication between you and your healthcare or hospice team to feel familiar with your loved one's illness and confident in the care you provide.

TIP #20
OVER CLARIFY

"It is wiser to find out than to suppose."

- Mark Twain

SIMILARLY, always ask for clarification for anything you may not understand. It's common to misinterpret or misunderstand information when under stress, especially when it's new. As an advanced nurse practitioner, I am thankful when my patients and families want and ask for clarification. This way, we know we are on the same page.

STRATEGY #1

Here are great examples to ask for clarification:

- "I'm not sure I understand exactly what you meant when you said _____. Would you mind saying this another way?"

- "I want to be sure I understood what you just said. When you said _____, did you mean _____?"

TIP #21
WRITE IT ALL DOWN

"The beauty of the written word is that it can be held close to the heart and read over and over again."

- Florence Littauer

WHEN MY GRANDDAD was dying at home on hospice, my Grandmother kept a notebook for daily notes. Several times a day, she would take the time to write about the happenings of the previous few hours. Every phone call, visitor, and conversation. Every hospice visit and new information they shared. Every meal. The weather. Everything and anything that had to do with my Granddad.

During an incredibly stressful and difficult time, my Grandmother struggled to remember even the smallest things. Being able to refer back to her notes gave her some peace of mind and became a safety net for her memories. After his death, my Grandmother's notebook became her therapy. Like a story, she was able to read, reflect, and reminisce on my Granddad's end-of-life journey with us all by his side.

Dedicate one or two notebooks to everything that has to do with your loved one. Write down everything and anything. From your healthcare team's observations, guidance, recommendations, and words of wisdom to all the happenings throughout the day. Include questions you have and the answers you find.

Write it all down.

With your head in the fog and daily stressors trying to keep you down, your memory will be limited. Your notes will help you recall important information, and, like my Grandma, they may unknowingly turn into therapeutic reflections.

TIP #22
ASK FOR HELP

"Refusing to ask for help when you need it is refusing someone the chance to be helpful."

- Ric Ocasek

WHY IS ASKING for help so hard for so many of us? Most of us learn from westernized cultures that to survive, we must be independent and self-sufficient. Therefore, asking for help makes us feel weak. We're afraid we'll be rejected and don't want to feel disappointed or ashamed. We don't think anyone truly *wants* to help us, nor do we think we deserve it. We believe that by asking for help, we aren't good enough. We're inept.

In reality, that's not how survival works. The way we survive is by working *together* as a community, hand-in-hand. Depending on one another – asking, receiving, and giving back when we can – is humanity's superpower. Some of us pretend we are Super-Human (myself included), but my friend, we are not. You are not. I am not. None of us are. So don't try to be.

If you try to take on every little responsibility, task, duty, and role yourself then you are in the process of hurling yourself toward caregiver burnout. Let go of any pride, shame, guilt, or stubbornness. Don't try to do everything yourself. Don't put it all on you. Learn to ask for help. You are not being needy, rude, or asking too much.

This caregiving journey is not a "one-man" job. It takes a village. People *want* to help you. They just don't always know how. Or they don't know what you need. Or they don't know what they should be doing...

Unless you speak up and tell them.

STRATEGY #1

HELP-ME LIST

Make a list of what you might need help with.

People will ask you all the time, "Let me know if there is anything I can do," or "What can I do for you?" or "If there is anything you need, I'm here."

The problem is you're never prepared with an answer when someone asks. Either because your mind has turned to mush or you feel like whatever you're asking is too much. But it's not too much, and they want to help. It is why they're asking.

So make a 'Help-Me List.' Either tell them what you need most or hand them your list and let them choose.

If you don't know where to start, here are some examples:

- Let someone bring you dinner.

- Let someone come over, wash your dishes, and clean the kitchen.
- Let someone come over and just be at the house or sit with your loved one while you step outside. Maybe you go for a walk, or a drive, or exercise, or sleep, or just breathe without having to worry about checking on them.
- Let someone come over and do your laundry.
- Let someone sit with you. Maybe just to listen. Or to talk. Or to share a story that has nothing to do with your current situation. Or to make you laugh. Or to lean on so you can cry.
- Let someone get you groceries.
- Let someone come clean your whole house! (Hey, why not?!)
- Let someone pick up your children from school or take them to practice.
- Let someone bring you pretty flowers that light up the house with fresh aromas.
- Let someone take you for a drive.
- Let other family members share caregiving responsibilities. Ask someone to manage your loved one's finances and bill payments. Ask someone to run errands or do the grocery shopping. Ask someone to set up and manage healthcare appointments.

STRATEGY #2

ADULT-CHILD COMPANION

Caregiving can take up most of your time and energy, leaving very little for others, your children included.

So, if you have children, consider appointing specific people to look after them. Designate one adult "support person" per child. Each adult's role is to act similar to that of a chaperone, a trusted person looking out for your child's safety and security. The adult should also act as a reliable companion and trusted friend, looking out for your child's emotional well-being.

The adult you choose should be someone who already has a bond and connection with your child. It should be someone who makes them feel comfortable, safe, and supported. This might be a relative such as an aunt or uncle, the parent of your child's close friend, a teacher, or a youth pastor. This extra pillar of support allows your children to receive the attention they need when your energy is limited.

Be sure to list specific phrases, topics, or words you do not want the adult to say or discuss with your children. Some issues may be sensitive or triggering. You know your child best.

STRATEGY #3

DESIGNATE A "LISTENER"

Designate a friend, family member, or someone close to you to be your "Listener." As caregivers, we aren't always looking for advice. Sometimes all we need is someone to talk to. Someone who will sit there in silence and just listen. Someone who will let us release all of our thoughts without needing to respond. Your designated Listener should understand that you aren't likely to call and reach out. Therefore, request that your Listener regularly check in on you by calling or visiting instead, maybe every evening.

TIP #23
LEARN TO SAY "YES"

"Having someone help you doesn't mean you failed. It just means you're not alone."

- Anonymous

LEARN TO SAY "YES!" Accept help from those who offer it. You don't have to be in this alone.

The act of receiving is difficult for many of us, myself included. We feel like we're burdening others. We feel guilty or ashamed. We're hard-headed and stubborn. Or maybe we're a combination of these.

So, let's try a little reverse psychology here to adjust your perspective. Think about how *you* feel when you help someone you care about. It usually feels good, doesn't it? It feels rewarding. Well, **Dear Caregiver**, others share this same feeling by helping you. So, lighten your load. Let go of some of the responsibility and welcome sharing it. You'll feel relieved, and so will they.

Saying "Yes" may not feel comfortable at first, but like anything, the more you do, the easier it gets. Now, go on and practice!

TIP #24
THE POWER OF "NO"

"When you say yes to something you don't want to do, here is the result: you hate what you are doing, you resent the person who asked you, and you hurt yourself."

- James Altucher

WHILE TIP #23 is all about the power of an appropriate "Yes," this tip is to remind you of the power of "No." It is fair and acceptable to say "No" to things that will not serve you or your loved one at this time.

For example, it's common for extended family, friends, and community members to call, email, text, and even come over to visit. They want to know the most recent updates on your loved one, or they may be simply checking in. Quite honestly, it's exhausting. While we caregivers tend to be people-pleasers, give yourself permission to let go of the idea that you have to respond in a hurry or even at all. Release any guilt, shame, or fear that might arise by reminding yourself you are not responsible for other people's feelings.

We live in a culture that makes us feel guilty for saying "No," which weakens this particular "No" muscle. The power of "No" takes courage, but it also brings freedom and peace to your life. Don't do anything that isn't right for you. "No" needs neither explanation nor justification. You have the right to protect and preserve your energy for what matters most.

STRATEGY #1

Here are examples of how to say "No" to what is not serving you right now.

- "Thank you so much for your thoughts/prayers/concerns/etc. We really appreciate it, but we are not having visitors right now."
- Do not answer the phone right now.
- Do not respond to that text message right now.
- Put your phone on "Do Not Disturb" or "Silent" Mode.
- Do not answer the door right now.
- Post a sign on the door that states you are not having visitors.
- Create a post on Facebook (Meta) saying you appreciate all the thoughts and well-wishes, but you'd like your space and privacy respected at this time.
- Create an automatic Email response that says, "Thank you for your emails. Please understand I will be taking time away from devices to rest, and so I will not be responding to emails at this time. We appreciate all your thoughts and prayers."
- Designate a Spokesperson who will communicate 1-8 (and more) on your behalf, so you won't need to worry about any of it. (See Tip #26)

Saying "No" is an act of self-preservation. The more you use your "No" muscle, the easier it gets. There is no rule book for these things.

You can choose to "do" this situation in any way that works for you. The goal is to protect your energy for the sake of yourself and all those you care for.

Your energy is limited right now. It is limited to caring for *yourself, your loved one,* and maybe your spouse and children. So, start practicing.

TIP #25
SEEK OUT YOUR RESOURCES

"You are not alone in the struggles of life. Entire cosmos are with you. It evolves through the way you face and overcome challenges of life. Use everything in your advantage."

- Amit Ray

CAREGIVING IS HARD WORK. It's constant work. It's draining work. It's physically, mentally, emotionally, spiritually, and financially exhausting and demanding. And so, this step is crucial.

Learn about other resources to help you. Research resources for personal care, home-health aide services, financial assistance, volunteer services, food assistance programs, caregiver support groups, bereavement support, spiritual support, used equipment, and so many others.

STRATEGY #1

Ask your healthcare team about additional resources they can offer such as...

- Home-health aide hours
- Volunteer services
- Nursing, social work, chaplain, bereavement visits, or any others
- Local or national financial assistance programs, organizations, or support services
- Respite care – which provides short-term care relief for caregivers (See Tip #32)

STRATEGY #2

Do an online search for local resources.

- Adult Day Care Centers
- Additional home-health service agencies
- Volunteer agencies
- Non-medical homecare services such as housecleaning, cooking, and companionship
- Sitters
- Meal delivery services
- Transportation Services
- Veterans Administration
- VA Caregiver Support Program
- VA Family Caregiver Assistance Program
- Local Area Agency on Aging
- Assisted Living Facility or Nursing Homes

Look for national groups.

- The U.S. Administration of Aging and the National Elder Locator are public service organizations to help connect older adults and families with support services and resources.

STRATEGY #3

Reach out to your local faith-group organizations or community center.

They often have support options, helpful information, or will help you find what you need.

STRATEGY #4

Get in touch with your Insurance Plan Representative.

Some insurance plans, such as Long-Term Care Insurance, often provide additional home-health care and personal care assistance.

STRATEGY #5

Research different technology tools that can assist you with your care.

- Virtual healthcare appointments
- Automated medicine dispenser
- Automated door locks
- Security alarms
- Security cameras
- Baby monitors
- Wearable emergency response systems
- Motion sensing devices
- GPS devices

TIP #26

APPOINT A SPOKESPERSON

"It's not your job to make people feel comfortable with the boundaries that you've set. It's not your job to accommodate other people's needs at your own expense."

- Michell Clark

IF YOU READ MY BOOK, *The Dying Process,* then you know the importance of designating someone you trust to be your "Spokesperson." A Spokesperson is someone who speaks to others on your behalf and is the only person you need to keep up to date. This person is likely another family member, a close friend, or someone you can rely on and trust.

As I mentioned in *The Dying Process,* as the caregiver, your phone, text, and email alerts are nonstop. Someone new is knocking at the door every day. Family, friends, and other community members expect regular updates about your loved one. Some may even request or expect personalized messages.

Because you are doing most (or all) of the caregiving, you feel responsible for keeping everyone in the loop. Some of you may try to neutralize the growing list of people to update by sending out "mass group text updates" or "mass email updates." From personal experience, being your own Spokesperson on top of caregiving is overwhelming and only drains you more.

Permit yourself to let go of this responsibility and shelter your energy. Feel encouraged to direct all communication to your designated Spokesperson from the start of your caregiving journey. Allow them to be your voice so that you can continue to show up and care for your loved one as you both deserve.

Tip #27

Designate An Accountability Partner

"An accountability partner is able to perceive what you can't see when blind spots and weaknesses block your vision. Such a person serves as a tool in God's hand to promote spiritual growth, and he or she watches out for your best interest."

- Charles Stanley

BEING a caregiver is like living in an out-of-body experience. The longer you stay in this caregiver role, the denser the fog you walk through. You can't see ahead of you. You can't see behind you. You can't even see your own two feet. The fog never totally clears, even after you've come to terms with being a caregiver, even after you find your new routine. You push, kick, and shove your way through the never-ending field of haze and smoke, never fully knowing what's happening around you, what's happening within you, or when it will end.

Let's face it; we aren't always the best judge of ourselves, even under normal circumstances. Sometimes it takes someone else saying,

"Hey, you don't seem like yourself," for us to realize, "Oh, you're right, I'm not." And these circumstances are far from normal.

It is for this reason that I recommend designating an Accountability Partner. This person might be a friend, family member, neighbor, colleague, or any other person you trust. As the name says, your Accountability Partner will be responsible for holding you accountable for maintaining the best version of yourself. They will act as your personal barometer, keeping your internal pressure stable and at baseline. They will measure where you are on a scale of "I'm doing great!" to "I've reached my Boiling Point," knowing that the closer you get to the latter, the closer you are to burning out.

STRATEGY #1

Create a personalized scale with your Accountability Partner to measure your stress levels.

SCALE EXAMPLE:

Doing Great —— Neutral —— Boiling Point

1 2 3 4 5 6 7 8 9 10

You cannot tell which way is up or forward when you get deep in the fog. The truth is, most of the time, you don't even know you're in it.

*You, **Dear Caregiver**,*
are well beyond your 25th hour.

You don't know that you need a break. You don't know that you haven't eaten. You don't know that you're snapping at others for little to no reason. You don't know you're someone no one wants to be around. You don't know that you're not living up to the best you or the best caregiver you can be.

And that's why we need others. People we can lean on - an Accountability Partner. Someone to say, "Hey, you look exhausted. Why don't I stay here while you get out of here? Go on a walk. Go for a drive. Go get some sleep. Just get away for a bit."

You will rely on your Accountability Partner to be your "when" person. They will tell you when you're getting too heated, tense, or worn and need to take a break. They will tell you when to step away from your caregiver role to sleep, shower, eat, or just get out of the house.

What's the other key to this?

Listen to them and follow their cue.

Tip #28
Get To Know Your Healthcare Support Team

"I can do things you cannot, you can do things I cannot; together we can do great things."

- Mother Teresa

No matter your loved one's current situation, get to know their healthcare team. They are a part of your team and will support you along this caregiving journey. Your loved one may have a primary care provider, homecare nurses, home-health aides, a social worker, specialists, or others.

If your loved one is on hospice, they will have a team of healthcare professionals who are each specially trained in end-of-life care. They are there to help you and your loved one in different ways throughout your loved one's dying process. This team typically includes nurses, physicians, nurse practitioners, social workers, hospice aides, bereavement counselors, non-denominational chaplains, volunteers, and administrative staff. Depending on the hospice, team members may vary slightly.

Get to know as many of your healthcare or hospice team members as possible. Welcome them into your home. Sit with them. Talk with them. Call them. Get to know who they are and what they do. Ask them as many questions as you can. Each team member offers their knowledge, wisdom, advice, and expertise.They have a *wealth* of knowledge just waiting to be tapped into.

So tap into it.

TIP #29
TALK TO A PRO'

"My therapist told me the way to achieve true inner peace is to finish what I start. So far today, I have finished 2 bags of M&M's and a chocolate cake. I feel better already."

- Dave Barry

I RECOMMEND TALKING to your own mental health professional. This mental health professional might be a trained psychologist, psychiatrist, therapist, counselor, social worker, or even a coach specializing in caregiving, your loved one's specific illness, death and dying, or grief and loss.

Keep in mind that not every mental health professional will be the right fit for you and vice versa. Sometimes it takes a few trials to find the person you mesh with the best. So don't be afraid to reach out and ask for a free 15-minute initial consultation with a therapist to get a feel for whether you might work well together.

From personal experience, I can attest to this. Throughout my life, I've sought out therapy and coaching for various reasons. On many occasions, it took several tries to find the right therapist or coach for me. It can be disheartening when you realize you need to keep searching but don't give up. The right person is out there, just waiting for you to connect. Your mental health is worth it, so keep trying.

Some mental health professionals will have in-person, virtual, or hybrid meeting options. In addition, they may offer single, family, or even group therapy options. Consider what type of therapy you prefer, or test out a variety to see what works best for you.

Like most things, I always like to go off of recommendations, therapists included. So ask friends, family, or your community if they can suggest a specific therapist they've used in the past. Similarly, ask your hospice team if they've heard of other families having luck with local therapists.

Keep in mind prices will vary depending on your country of origin, health coverage, and type of mental health professional. So do your research. Call your insurance company and the mental health professional of interest to discuss costs.

In addition, if your loved one is receiving hospice services, ask to meet with specific team members who specialize in family coping, death and dying, and grief and loss. These team members include the hospice social worker, bereavement counselor, and chaplain. Their services are free and included in your hospice benefit.

Tip #30
Connect With People

"Connection is why we're here. We are hardwired to connect with others, it's what gives purpose and meaning to our lives, and without it there is suffering."

- Brené Brown

DURING THIS TIME, connecting and maintaining your relationships outside your caregiver role is essential.

Talk with others.
Laugh with others.
Cry with others.
Play with others.
Share with others.
Be vulnerable with others.
Surround yourself with people who get you, love you, light up your spirit, and lift your heart.

At our core, we humans are social creatures. Scientists believe our brains are naturally wired to form bonds and connect with others. We need human connection to not only survive but thrive. According to "Maslow's Hierarchy of Needs," the three most basic human needs are physiological, safety, and love and belonging.

Physiological needs include food, water, shelter, and the air we breathe. Safety needs include our health, employment, education, and personal security. Love and belonging needs include our friendships, family, intimacy, and our sense of connection with others. These core needs are an essential part of our overall well-being. We feel seen, heard, valued, and whole when we connect with others. Other benefits include...

- Improved overall quality of life and life satisfaction
- Increased resilience and ability to overcome challenges
- Improved mental health and self-esteem
- Improved immune system and lifespan
- Improved ability to cope with grief
- Increased confidence in our support system

I don't know about you, but I'd say those are a some pretty good reasons not to be a hermit. So go on now, connect! Bond! Reach out! Be vulnerable! It's not a scary as you think and will give your heart strings the lovin' it's been needing. I promise.

STRATEGY #1

Family members can be an easy and convenient source of support and comfort. As a family, you can both relate to the shared experience of your loved one's health decline. Together you can share old stories, reminisce on meaningful memories, and create new family bonding experiences that bring you closer together.

Strategy #2

Talk to a friend.

Friends can remind you of life before caregiving. They can offer their ears or a shoulder to cry on. They make you laugh when you need it most or offer comfort through silence.

Friends also provide an opportunity to be social again – to get out of the house, be around other people, and step away from your caregiver mentality.

Friends are a gift. They know you inside and out and tend to know just what you need. They give you the space to be vulnerable and free.

TIP #31
GET COMMUNITY SUPPORT

"Heroes didn't leap tall buildings or stop bullets with an outstretched hand; they didn't wear boots and capes. They bled, and they bruised, and their superpowers were as simple as listening, or loving. Heroes were ordinary people who knew that even if their own lives were impossibly knotted, they could untangle someone else's. And maybe that one act could lead someone to rescue you right back."

- Jodi Picoult

JOIN A COMMUNITY SUPPORT GROUP. This tip goes hand-in-hand with the importance of human connection, detailed in Tip #30.

There is something deeply impactful about connecting with others going through similar experiences, even if those people are strangers. Support groups offer a place to share your problems, worries, or thoughts and, at the same time, receive invaluable feedback from others who can relate to similar situations. It is a place where you, too, have the opportunity to lend your advice in the hopes of helping someone else. While you may start as strangers, your vulnerability will serve to build bonds, connections, and genuine friendships.

Our **Death.Care.Coach Facebook Community Support Group** welcomes anyone looking for just that. We offer our ears, sincere words, support, guidance, education, and encouragement worldwide.

Join us at
www.facebook.com/groups/death.care.coach

Other local and online support groups often focus on caregivers and grief support. If you are associated with any particular religious, spiritual, or cultural group, these are other avenues that frequently offer support groups with love, compassion, and empathy.

TIP #32
USE RESPITE CARE

"Rest and self-care are so important. When you take time to replenish your spirit, it allows you to serve others from the overflow. You cannot serve from an empty vessel."

- Eleanor Brown

IF YOUR LOVED one is on hospice, take advantage of your opportunity to use respite care if or when you need a break.

What is respite care?

Respite care provides short-term relief for caregivers. With respite care, your loved one continues to receive the care and support they need from health professionals while you get to rest. Utilize your hospice social worker as a great resource to help set this up for you and your loved one. Healthcare facilities, including assisted living facilities, nursing homes, or hospitals, typically provide respite care. In addition, it may be possible to have respite care at home or in an adult day care center. While under the hospice benefit, Medicare only covers up to a certain number of respite days per year. However, your loved one may be eligible for more respite coverage through other local or national assistance programs.

Suppose your loved one is not on hospice. In that case, other resources such as your local Area Agency on Aging, local adult day service organizations, local respite care organizations, or your State Health Insurance Assistance Program (SHIP) may offer other care relief options.

TIP #33
TRY MEDITATION

"Quiet the mind and the soul will speak."

- Ma Jaya Sati Bhagavati

MEDITATION IS A POWERFUL PRACTICE. However, many people tell themselves they "can't" meditate or are "bad" at meditating.

My mind constantly wandered when I began testing the water with meditation. First, I'd think about my back hurting. Then I'd remember I forgot to make a phone call yesterday. Then I'd think about what I was going to eat for breakfast. Then I'd remember my back was still hurting. Then I'd think about how bad I was at this whole meditation thing.

Yet after years of meditating, I now know it is impossible to be "bad" at meditation. It is a practice, like anything else. And the benefits are *overwhelming*. Meditation teaches you to calm your body and quiet your mind.

Several free meditation phone apps, music apps (like Spotify or Pandora), YouTube channels, and other online resources can walk you through the practice. Some are short, and some are long. If you are new to meditation, I recommend short, five to ten-minute trials to get comfortable. While there are many ways to meditate, I have found this simple practice works well for beginners.

STRATEGY #1

STEP 1
Go to a quiet space. Inside or outside.

STEP 2
Set an alarm nearby for anywhere from one to 20 minutes. (Or more if you'd like!)

STEP 3
Sit or lie in any comfortable position that feels good.

STEP 4
Close your eyes.

STEP 5
Take a slow deep breath through your nose, filling your belly first, then your chest.

STEP 6
When you can't take in any more air, briefly pause. Hold your breath for one to three seconds.

STEP 7
Slowly release. Exhale all the air through your mouth, leaving your belly first, then your chest.

STEP 8
Repeat steps five through seven twice more.

STEP 9

Begin to steady your breath to a comfortable inhale and exhale. Notice where the air is moving with each breath. Maybe you follow the air as it enters your nostrils and fills your belly. Then you follow it back out from your belly, through your chest, and out your nostrils.

STEP 10

Keep your attention on your breath.

STEP 11

Each inhale.

STEP 12

Each exhale.

STEP 13

If you begin to notice yourself thinking about something, silently say to yourself, "Thinking," and then let the thought fade away.

STEP 14

Then refocus your attention back on your breath, following the air in and out.

STEP 15

Keep your eyes closed until your alarm has gone off.

STEP 16

When your alarm goes off, open your eyes to turn it off.

STEP 17

Do a quick self check-in.

How do you feel?

How was that for you?

In what way(s) do you feel different?

Does your body feel any lighter?

Does your mind feel calmer?

If you were thinking the entire time your eyes were closed, don't worry. You can expect to think because, hey, that's what our brains do!

You are practicing meditation every time you notice a thought, let it go without judgment, and refocus your attention back on your breath. You might not feel any different, at least not right away. But, over time, you'll notice your thoughts and quiet your mind more easily.

There is extensive research showing the tremendous benefits of daily meditation when it comes to mental and physical well-being.

So give it a try and keep at it.

TIP #34
BE MINDFUL

"The body always leads us home ... if we can simply learn to trust sensation and stay with it long enough for it to reveal appropriate action, movement, insight, or feeling."

- Pat Ogden

IT WASN'T until I hit a "rock bottom" point in my life that I found mindfulness. During that time, I had been going through several major life changes. I was working through my own grief and loss journey (which I now know is lifelong), adapting to a career change, and adjusting to a new home. I was feeling the effects of chronic stress, and it was taking a serious toll on my life. I wasn't sleeping. I was experiencing chronic pain issues. I was depressed and irritable, contributing to strain on my relationships. I couldn't seem to focus or get any kind of work done. I had to find a way to dig myself out of the hole.

A friend of mine introduced me to both mindfulness and meditation practices. I was skeptical, of course. But I was also desperate. I had no idea where to start, but I thought, "Hey, what the heck... I've got nothing to lose." So I searched and downloaded the first three mindfulness apps I could find for my phone and dove right in.

My sleep improved so much, to my amazement, that I started looking forward to climbing into bed at night. My low back pain slowly faded. My mood lightened. I was happier and more cheerful, and my relationships dramatically improved. It was like magic.

Since then, I've continued to practice mindfulness and meditation. These practices have improved the quality of my life in such a profound way that they are something I prioritize as part of my daily morning routine.

I hope you, too, will give it a shot because, hey, you've got nothing to lose and everything to gain.

Mindfulness is a thoughtful practice that reduces stress, depression, anxiety, and insomnia. While often done during meditation, you can practice being mindful at any point throughout your day. "To be mindful" is to become consciously aware of both your body and mind. Like a "third wheel," you're an observer, except you're observing yourself this time. It's like a new awakening as you begin to tune in to your thoughts and feelings physically and mentally, never judging whatever you find.

By practicing mindfulness, you are learning to be more self-aware. The more self-aware, the more clearly you'll see, know, and understand yourself. In turn, you'll be able to recognize your needs more readily and nurture yourself accordingly.

These strategies may help you incorporate mindfulness into your daily life.

STRATEGY #1

BECOME AWARE OF YOUR BODY

STEP 1

To do this, spend a few moments doing a body scan from your head down to your toes. Take a few seconds to notice how each body part is feeling.

STEP 2

Rather than becoming upset with a particular sensation you are experiencing, such as tightness in your lower back, simply notice its *presence.*

STEP 3

Take a few extra seconds to breathe into that area.

STEP 4

With each exhale, imagine the tightness leaving your body and your muscles loosening.

STEP 5

Continue to mindfully move down your body parts, doing the same for any sensation that may need a little extra attention and release.

STRATEGY #2

BECOME AWARE OF YOUR THOUGHTS

Because you are constantly on the move throughout your day, thoughts fly in and out of your mind unnoticed. Begin to incorporate three moments in your day to stop whatever you're doing intentionally and check in on these thoughts. Observe what these thoughts are telling you. What you say to yourself matters. Notice how these thoughts make you feel.

Under stress, our brains often magnify the bad, which only intensifies anxiety. However, by paying attention to this inner chatter, you can begin talking back to the negative voice in your head by introducing a positive thought, thereby relieving stress. (See Tip #55 for more on this.)

TIP #35
REMEMBER TO BREATHE

"Breathe. Let go. And remind yourself that this very moment is the only one you know you have for sure.

- Oprah Winfrey

IF YOU'VE EVER BEEN to a yoga class, you will continuously hear the instructor remind you to *"Come back to your breath."* Your quads, glutes, and calves are burning and trembling in whatever yoga pose you're in, but somehow you're supposed to remember to *"Just breathe."* Or they've got you in a figure-four pose (pigeon pose), trying to open up your hips, but your hips are screaming at you. Still, it's, *"Just breathe."*

Why is the breath so powerful?

Breathwork has evolved over the years, with many different techniques arising all the time. In its purest form, our breath keeps our bodies alive, bringing oxygen into our lungs to circulate with each inhale and allowing carbon dioxide waste to leave our bodies with each exhale. Research has shown that breathwork can be healing, therapeutic, and transformative when we intentionally focus on our breath, becoming consciously aware of each inhale and exhale.

On a physical level, we can use our breath to influence our nervous system. For example, when stressed or anxious, we can use our breath to activate the part of our nervous system that helps us feel relaxed and calm. On a mental level, we can use our breath to call us back to the present moment. During stressful times, our minds often wander and quickly lose focus. When we focus on our breath, we can learn to let go of distractions and worries and return to what is right here and now. On a spiritual level, we can use our breath to connect to our higher Self or the Universe by intentionally breathing energy within and all around us. If you aren't digging any of this so far, realize your breath is what keeps you going.

So, **Dear Caregiver,**
If you do anything, remember to breathe. Breathe in. Breathe out. And let it go.

Deep Breathing, or "Belly Breathing," is a purposeful, well-researched practice that has several health benefits helping to lower stress, anxiety, and depression. Follow these simple instructions for two to four minutes at least once daily.

STRATEGY #1

STEP 1
The easiest way to start is to find a place to lie comfortably flat on your back.

STEP 2

Place a pillow under your head and neck and another under bent knees to support your low back.

STEP 3
Place one hand on your belly and the other over your chest.

STEP 4
Close your eyes if that feels comfortable.

STEP 5
Take a slow deep breath through your nose, filling your belly.

You should feel the hand on your belly rise with your inhale. However, the hand on your chest should remain relatively still.

STEP 6
Through pursed lips on your exhale, tighten your core muscles as if you are pushing air out of your belly.

You should feel the hand on your belly fall back down while the hand on your chest remains relatively still.

STEP 7
Continue inhaling to fill your belly and exhaling empty your belly for several minutes.

TIP #36
A GOOD MORNING STRETCH

"You'll never change your life until you change something you do daily. The secret of your success is found in your daily routine."

- John C. Maxwell

I CARED for an older couple in their early 80s, Tom and Jill. In many ways, they were caregivers for each other's ailments. It was always interesting how they clearly shared some mystical, energetic connection. When Tom had back pain, Jill developed back pain. When Jill had an achy knee, Tom had an achy knee. When Tom had bowel troubles, Jill had bowel troubles. It was almost as if the stress from one spouse would leap over and into the other. Somehow, I convinced them to start a simple morning routine they could practice together. Before getting out of bed in the morning, they would each perform a few simple leg and shoulder exercises and stretches. To their surprise, many of the chronic issues they had both been experiencing faded away, never to return.

We all know the feeling of waking up to a big "Good Morning" stretch before climbing out of bed. It's like itching a scratch we'd been ignoring all night. Stretch your muscles anywhere from five to twenty minutes (or more) every day.

We often hold onto mental and emotional stress throughout our bodies. Stress can manifest in our bodies as pain, tightness, body or joint aches, abdominal issues, headaches, and more. Stretching is a simple way to move your body and release built-up tension. Gentle yoga and Tai Chi are other light stretching exercises that can improve your overall well-being. Incorporating these practices help you to feel more centered, relieve stress, and cultivate feelings of peace.

TIP #37
BRAIN DUMP WITH A JOURNAL

"I can shake off everything as I write; my sorrows disappear, my courage is reborn."

- Anne Frank

THERE WILL BE times in your caregiving journey when you may be unaware or unable to describe how you are genuinely doing. You might even feel emotionless. The caregiving journey has its highs, lows, and long-stagnant plateaus. Each day falls into the next.

As caregivers, we often ignore or bottle our emotions, which unfortunately begin to consume every bit of us. They invade our brains and consequently drain our spirits. Because caregiving can feel isolating and lonely, finding an outlet to express ourselves can be challenging.

While we've talked about journaling earlier, its significance stands here as its own tip. Journaling has impressive long-term benefits, such as decreasing depression and anxiety, improving relationships, boosting the immune system, and improving sleep. It also enhances our ability to cope with stressful situations.

For starters, journaling can act as our outlet. When we don't know who to turn to, a journal can offer us a safe space to vent. We're able to be vulnerable without fear of being judged. A journal allows us to dump our chaotic thoughts and feelings onto paper. It's a place to remove the mess from our brains so we can begin to make sense of our emotions. It lets us collect ourselves, organize our thought processes, and understand what we are experiencing.

Additionally, we can further reflect on our lives and everything we are going through. Doing this gives us the ability to manage our situation better. Seeing your emotions on paper takes away the power they have over you. So give it a try. Take a pen to paper and write. Whatever comes out, let it flow.

STRATEGY #1

If you don't know where to start, here are a few simple journal reflections that may help you find the emotional release you're looking for…

- If I could choose one emotion for how I am feeling right now, what would it be?
- What part of my body feels the strongest today?
- What part of my body feels like it needs rest or more love?
- What went well today?
- What could have gone better today? What can I do to improve this tomorrow?
- How can I practice giving myself more grace today?
- What has made me stronger today?
- What is a small win that I can celebrate today?
- If [name your loved one] could talk to me, what would they say to me right now?
- What is one thing I did for myself today? (Writing in this journal could be that one thing.)
- What is one adjustment I would like to make to my morning or evening routine?

- What is one long-term goal I will work towards?
- What is one thing I have learned from all that I am going through?
- What surprised me most today?
- (After going through these questions, ask this question again.) If I could choose one emotion for how I am feeling at this moment, what would it be?

TIP #38
PRACTICE GRATITUDE

"Acknowledging the good that you already have in your life is the foundation for all abundance."

- Eckhart Tolle

GRATITUDE CAN MEAN something different to everyone. The term gratitude originates from the Latin expression, gratia, which means grace, kindness, thanks, or gratefulness.

For me, *gratitude* is a deep sense of thankfulness and appreciation for anything meaningful in my life - the opportunity to live is one of them. Every morning I think of three things I am grateful for. Sometimes, they are memories or experiences that come from the past. Sometimes, they are from the present, feeling blessed for all I have. Sometimes, they are for the hopeful future. Sometimes I feel grateful for tangible things; the roof over my head, the food on my table, the body I live in. But I often feel blessed for the intangible things; my relationships with family and friends, the lessons I've learned, and the experiences I've had and will have. In this way, I allow myself to see the goodness that life offers and can feel connected to something greater than myself.

Even when life throws really hard stuff at us, even when life tests us, there is still an opportunity for us to choose gratitude. Some of you might be thinking, "How on earth can you expect me to be grateful right now?" Under challenging circumstances, it's not always natural for us to *feel* grateful. Forcing ourselves to be thankful has the potential to dismiss or minimize the pain, hurt, or sadness we are experiencing.

Having said that, there are still ways to find the good, even in the midst of hardship. By staying open and looking for opportunities, you'll begin to cultivate a genuine appreciation for what you have rather than agonize over what you lack.

Being grateful takes practice. It takes time to train your mind to see the good rather than the bad. But with consistency and open-mindedness, you'll find true gratitude breeds positive feelings and happiness. Even on my roughest, messiest, darkest days, gratitude brings me back to home base. It grounds me with feelings of safety, peace, and inspiration. I hope it can do the same for you.

STRATEGY #1

Every morning think of three to five things you are grateful for. If you need help knowing where to start, try these easy gratitude prompts.

- I am grateful for [person] because...
- I am grateful for [thing] because...
- I am grateful for this moment because...
- I am grateful for this situation because it has taught me...
- I am grateful for my body because...
- I am grateful to have...
- I am grateful for this experience because... (Did you learn

something? Are you stronger in some way? Did you meet someone? Did it lead you to do something new or unexpected?)

- I am grateful for the help of [person, place, thing] because…

TIP #39
REPEAT POSITIVE AFFIRMATIONS

"Attitude is a choice. Happiness is a choice. Optimism is a choice. Kindness is a choice. Giving is a choice. Respect is a choice. Whatever choice you make makes you. Choose wisely."

- Roy T. Bennett

POSITIVE AFFIRMATIONS ARE optimistic phrases or statements you repeat to help combat negative thoughts and inspire positive transformation in your life. From inspiring change to boosting self-confidence, with positive affirmations, you'll adopt an attitude of optimism and improve your outlook on life. Using positive affirmations to break old negative thought patterns takes repetition. The more you repeat positive affirmations, the more you'll personify its meaning.

Every morning, I write down five to ten positive affirmations. Sometimes they are healing and therapeutic. Other times they are motivating and encouraging. Adopting positive affirmations has driven me to become a better and better version of myself - healing my heart and nurturing my inner soul. Incorporating this daily habit has also helped me realize that I *am* the director of my movie. I am the captain of my ship. I am the star of my show. No one else. I have the choice to embrace and *be* the person *I* want to be. I am who I am and not the way others see me.

STRATEGY #1

Make up your own, or try repeating these positive self-affirmations to yourself every morning. Then, repeat them once during the day and again before bed.

For the biggest impact, look at yourself in the mirror while reading them out loud.

- My heart is full of love and thankfulness.
- I am doing the best I can every day. I am enough. I am capable. I am loved.
- No matter what today brings, I will choose to see the good.
- I am rejuvenated and full of energy.
- Today, I choose to speak to myself and others with love and grace.
- I am radiating positive energy and strength today.
- I am proud of myself.
- I am resilient. I am growing stronger every day.
- I am exactly where I am meant to be.
- I am a wise being. The answers are always within me.
- I am open to opportunities that help me learn, grow, and evolve.

TIP #40
RECONNECT WITH YOUR IDENTITY

"Today you are you! That is truer than true!
There is no one alive who is you-er than you!
Shout loud, 'I am lucky to be what I am!...'"

- Dr. Seuss

IN OTHER WORDS...

Reconnect with YOU.

Do something for You... Every. Single. Day. You constantly give yourself to others but are much more than a caregiver. Caregiving does not define you. *You* choose what defines you.

Remind yourself of who you are by doing something that aligns with your most authentic Self. Do something that aligns with your morals and values. Do something that makes you feel good inside. Do something that makes you say, *"This is me."* This activity should have nothing to do with caring for your loved one and everything to do with *you*.

STRATEGY #1

Start by asking yourself these questions.

- What do you see when you envision your most authentic self? Who are you? What's your story? What are the things that make you who you are?
- What brings you joy?
- What reminds you of life before caregiving?
- What did you do before you started caring for your loved one?
- What helps you feel centered? Grounded?
- What sparks the kid in you?
- What lights you up!?

Many of the tips in this book may already bring you comfort and a sense of Self.

If so, great! Continue to act on these things.

STRATEGY #2

If you are struggling to remember what makes you YOU, here are a few other engaging activities and hobbies you might relate to...

- Read a book.
- Watch a movie.
- Have dinner with a friend.
- Bake a cake or cookies.
- Draw, color, or paint.
- Read or browse a bookstore.

- Go to your place of worship.
- Knit, crochet, or sew.
- Dance or sing.
- Go hiking, fishing, or swimming.
- Play a video, table, or card game.
- Garden.
- See a show or musical.
- Write a letter, poem, or song.
- Go for a run or bike ride.
- Watch the sunset.
- Go shopping or get your hair done.
- Scrapbook or collage.
- Paint

STRATEGY #3

PLAN YOUR FUTURE

You've planned for your future your entire life. Though caregiving may not have been a part of your original plan, here you are.

Despite this, caregiving is almost certainly not your forever. There is life after caregiving, and it's time to start thinking about what that looks like for you.

Ask yourself questions.

- What do you want your ideal life to look like, feel like, and be like?
- What do you want to do with the rest of your life? Think as if you are your future self.
- What are you doing?
- Where are you living?

- Who are you living and interacting with? What do you look like?
- How do you feel?

Once you have a vision of what your future self and future life are like, begin thinking about the steps you will take to get there. What is the one thing you can do to get an inch closer to the future life you dream of?

Tip #41
It's Time... It's "Me-Time"

(AKA...TAKE BREAKS!)

"When you recover or discover something that nourishes your soul and brings joy, care enough about yourself to make room for it in your life."

- Jean Shinoda Bolen

HANNAH WAS the primary caregiver for her husband with early-onset Alzheimer's Disease. Alzheimer's is a type of Dementia that slowly affects brain function. After diagnosis, most people will live anywhere from three to 11 years. Hannah's husband was going on his 15th year. He was bed-bound, non-verbal, and needed total care. It required Hannah to be available 24 hours a day, seven days a week.

Knowing this back story, you might expect Hannah would be losing both her hair and her mind. You'd probably expect her to be depressed, worn out, and barely surviving. Yet, she wasn't. She was thriving. Every visit, I couldn't help but notice the content smile on her face, the pep in her step, and the glow that seemed to radiate around her. Her secret, you ask?

"Me-Time."

While her husband's mind was still strong, he made Hannah promise to carve out time for herself daily. Having developed a routine over the years, she incorporated and prioritized frequent breaks. Hannah knew this was a marathon, not a sprint. While she loved and cared deeply about her husband, they both wanted her to continue thriving.

We've said it before, but it deserves to stand on its own here in this tip. Take breaks daily. Part of the work is rest. So give yourself permission to take space and rest. Whether it's five to ten minutes scattered throughout your day or a few longer breaks at a time.

You must *come up for air.*
You must *take a step back.*
You must *step away.*

Giving yourself the *green light* to step away from your caregiver role and the loved one you are caring for gives you the chance to reset, refuel, and recharge. Rest to rejuvenate. Rest allows you to look at the bigger picture and remind yourself that you *can* and will get through this. Give yourself the "Me-Time" you deserve.

Dear Caregiver,
No excuses.

STRATEGY #1

Ask a friend, a neighbor, a family member or relative, a volunteer, a spiritual community member, your Accountability Partner, or someone you trust for their time. Allow them to stay with your loved one so that you can rest.

STRATEGY #2

Create a routine that allows you to step away.

Refer to Tip #1, Strategy #2, as an example.

STRATEGY #3

Create a "sanctuary" or a safe space where you can go to find peace and comfort. Set this space up in a way that welcomes you. This sanctuary might look different for everyone. Some of you might include a cozy chair, a warm blanket, and candles. Others might create this space outdoors in the fresh open air by a river or a tree. Whatever this space is, be sure it is one that helps you relax and disconnect or clear your mind and reflect.

TIP #42
SEEK FINANCIAL ASSISTANCE

Don't be afraid to ask questions. Don't be afraid to ask for help when you need it. I do that every day. Asking for help isn't a sign of weakness, it's a sign of strength. It shows you have the courage to admit when you don't know something, and to learn something new.

- Barack Obama

MANY OF YOU may work or have a career outside of caring for your loved one. Because caregiving for a loved one at the end of life often requires full- or part-time hours, balancing your energy between your job and caregiver role is critical. This can be a challenge for many of us who require a steady income in order to take care of ourselves and our families. So seek out financial advice and assistance using some of these strategies.

Strategy #1

REQUEST TIME OFF WORK

If it is possible for you and your family, using both paid and unpaid time off of work may allow you to focus your energy on caring for your loved one.

Many jobs offer PTO (paid time off), vacation or holiday time, sick time, and family leave time from work.

For example, in the United States, the Family and Medical Leave Act (FMLA) was created to give employees up to 12 weeks of unpaid time off work per year without the risk of losing their job and health insurance benefits.

FMLA allows employees to balance work, life, and family needs, which includes caring for a loved one with serious health conditions.

Strategy #2

PAYING THE CAREGIVER BY FAMILY CONTRACT

Some of you may leave your normal day job because your caregiving duties require you to be with your loved one around the clock. In these situations, there may still be ways to get paid.

Some families construct a contract between the family member taking on the caregiver role and the rest of the family. This contract clearly states a specific income to be paid to the family caregiver. The caregiver then gets paid directly by their other family members.

A lawyer can be useful when writing and reviewing this type of contract.

STRATEGY #3

GOVERNMENT RESOURCES

Tax Benefits and Loans

Because family caregivers make up millions of dollars otherwise spent on unnecessary healthcare costs, many countries have special programs or government benefits dedicated to paying family caregivers.

For example, family caregivers may qualify for certain tax benefits or claim tax-deductible expenses if their loved one is the dependent. If your loved one qualifies as your dependent, you may also be able to set up a Flexible Spending Account (FSA) to pay for their health expenses. A Multiple Support Declaration may also assist families with tax benefits if care costs are shared among multiple family members.

Your local Area Agency on Aging or your State Health Insurance Assistance Program (SHIP) may further assist you with other government benefits that may apply.

Your loved one may also be eligible for different government loans. For example, various loan programs offered through the U.S. Department of Housing and Urban Development will assist with home renovation and repair costs.

The Social Security Administration

If your loved one is a widow or widower, they may be able to claim benefits from the Social Security Administration (SSA). However, have your loved one apply for survivor benefits sooner rather than later since missed claims aren't guaranteed. In addition, the SSA may require certain documents to process claims.

Medicaid Assistance

Most states in the United States have Medicaid programs that give money to qualified older adults to help them pay for caregivers. Qualifications and requirements differ in each state. However, some states allow a spouse, guardian, or another family member to be paid as their caregiver. If your loved one is covered under Medicaid, they may qualify for self-directed services funds, which can assist with caregiving expenses.

Other State Programs

In the United States, some states may have other programs to help pay family caregivers, especially those that do not meet Medicaid requirements.

Your local Medicaid Office or Area Agency on Aging are two resources to find out more information.

Military Veterans Programs

In the United States, there are different assistance plans that veterans may qualify for. These programs offer financial assistance to pay caregivers and home-health services. Visit the U.S. Department of Veterans Affairs website to search for your local office and benefits.

Long-Term Care Insurance

If your loved one has long-term care insurance, some policies will help pay for the costs of home-health care and personal care assistance.

Other Government Benefits

Governments outside the U.S. may have benefits to help pay family caregivers.

In Canada, for example, Employment Insurance benefits assist family caregivers by allowing them to take paid time off work for extended periods to care for sick adults or children. In addition, employer benefits and other Employee Assistance Programs may offer additional resources to assist with paid caregiving.

Similarly, in the United Kingdom, the government has developed a Carer's Allowance, which allows family (or other) carers to receive a certain amount of money weekly and other carer benefits.

STRATEGY #4

LEGAL AND FINANCIAL ASSISTANCE

Lawyers, financial advisors, or accountants may be helpful professionals to seek advice or assist with financial questions and concerns.

STRATEGY #5

SOCIAL WORKER ASSISTANCE

Reach out to your hospice or healthcare team's social worker to discuss other programs or benefits they may be aware of. Your social worker is a great resource and someone who can help you find contacts, opportunities, and other local or national paid benefits. In addition, they can help you fill out and file applications, paperwork, and other forms that may need to be submitted.

TIP #43
SEEK SPIRITUAL SUPPORT

"The spiritual journey is the unlearning of fear and the acceptance of love."

- Marianne Williamson

BY DEFINITION, spirituality is "the quality of being concerned with the human spirit or soul as opposed to material or physical things." On an individual level, that definition is relatively broad and open to interpretation, leaving the concept rather limitless. Spirituality is a universal human experience, *yet we all perceive and participate in it differently.*

For me, spirituality is an inner knowing that there is something far greater than what we know now. While I can't begin to explain what that is, my life experiences have led me to trust, believe, and have faith that there is more to all of this. And given that, my life, and all other life, has meaning and purpose. We are all deeply connected on a level well beyond the known.

To some of you, spirituality may feel similar to my vision. To some of you, spirituality may directly relate to religion or place of worship.

To some of you, spirituality may be your relationship with God(s) or other higher powers. To some of you, spirituality may be your connection with nature, body movement, or the arts. To some of you, spirituality may feel sacred, majestic, transcendent, holy, divine, heavenly, or blessed.

For some, prayer, meditation, or ritual may be spiritually comforting. Prayer can be a wish, an expression of thanks, speaking your thoughts, or a request for help. You may or may not direct your prayer toward any one thing, person, or higher power. If it feels right, I encourage you to pray, meditate, or partake in other reassuring rituals.

If you associate or have a relationship with any particular religious, spiritual, or cultural group leader, reach out to them for guidance and support. Often, they will come to your home and sit with you, your loved one, and any others who may find comfort in their presence and words. Your hospice chaplain is another accessible resource for non-denominational spiritual counseling and comfort. Ask to meet with them in your home or on the phone at your convenience.

Your spiritual health and emotional state are linked. Find solace in continuing your spiritual journey or practices and welcome the positive feelings of peace, love, gratitude, contentment, and wonder they unlock.

TIP #44
CELEBRATE SMALL WINS

"It's the small wins on the long journey that we need in order to keep our confidence, joy and motivation alive."

- Brendon Burchard

FRANK WAS NOT the caregiving type, but when his mother was slowly dying of cancer, he decided to take a step back from his elite finance job and take a giant step up to the plate. While I watched him struggle occupationally and socially, his real battles were physical and emotional. Frank and his mother were very close. They had the typical mother-son bond you think of, the kind that can be hard to come between. He was not only the only son but also the only child.

While grappling with his mother's impending death and never having been a caregiver, he managed to find his way. He would "fail" twenty times a day – from learning to change an older woman's soiled briefs to figuring out how to situate her comfortably enough that she wouldn't be in pain from the pressure wound that had developed on her buttocks. It was a *lot*, but Frank kept going.

I arrived one afternoon with him smiling from ear to ear. Frank told me how he'd just figured out a trick to changing his mother's clothes without having to shift her back and forth five times before getting it right. He was thrilled and deserved this small celebration for the day. After that, every week I'd return - Frank sharing his new accomplishments and bigger smiles each visit. I watched as his initial distress transformed into determination, each "win" pushing him through each day.

In stressful times, it's much easier to "see" the bad than to see the good. Celebrate any win, big or small, as often as you can. These are the little moments that keep us going. While we may not be doing everything right, these are the mini reminders that we aren't getting everything wrong either. These are the tiny triumphs that propel us forward each day.

Dear Caregiver,
Every small win will give you the motivation to keep going. Every small victory builds belief in yourself – that you are capable. The more you praise and celebrate the small stuff in life, the more you stack the odds on your side to get through the big stuff.

STRATEGY #1

For example…

- You changed your loved one's soiled underpants for the first time.

Win!

- You changed your loved one's soiled underpants for the hundredth time.

Win!

- You helped your loved one find a comfortable position.

Win!

- You got out of bed this morning.

Win!

- You made it through another day.

Win!

- You left the house this morning to catch a five-minute break.

Win!

Even if it's small, even if it's silly, even if it seems insignificant, honor it. You deserve to be celebrated.

TIP #45
BE YOUR OWN BEST CHEERLEADER

"Life will always have its ups & downs, how you engage with those moments is what matters. Choosing to believe you are valuable & capable, regardless of what's going on is how to quiet harmful self-talk, stay positive, and bend reality in your favor."

- Cory Allen

WHEN WAS the last time you sat down and gave yourself credit for how much you've done, how far you've come, or how much you've grown? When was the last time you celebrated how incredible you truly are?If you can't applaud yourself and everything you are doing, then who will? You are a gift to this world. It's time you recognize your worth.

You got this!

STRATEGY #1

Repeat these positive affirmations out loud, in your head, or on paper.

- "Yes I can!"
- "I am learning from every mistake I make."
- "I am doing what I can today."
- "I got out of bed this morning!"
- "I am doing a great job."
- "I am proud of the way I am caring for _____."
- "I am proud of myself for keeping my boundaries and taking care of myself, too."
- "I am resilient. I have been through so much and I am stronger and wiser because of it."
- "I have come so far."
- "I am just really, really proud of myself."
- "I am working on my fears.

TIP #46
HIRE A HOMECARE ASSISTANT

"You gain strength, courage, and confidence by every experience in which you really stop to look fear in the face. You are able to say to yourself, 'I lived through this horror. I can take the next thing that comes along.' You must do the thing you think you cannot do."

- Eleanor Roosevelt

IF FINANCIALLY ABLE, and especially if you are not available 24 hours a day, hire a homecare assistant such as a home-health aide or private caregiver. This will give you some freedom, flexibility, and rest by releasing some of your caregiver duties.

When hiring someone to help care for your loved one, there are several things you want to be sure of. First, hire someone you know you can trust. This might come from the combination of background checks, references, and an overall gut feeling. Always trust your gut. Second, feel confident in their ability to provide quality care. This also comes from reference checks and observing hands-on care. Lastly, ensure you are both on the same page regarding specific caregiving duties you'd like them to perform. Establish this by creating your own written list or a routine to follow.

Even when hiring a homecare assistant through a company, I recommend hand-selecting the person. Interview potential candidates yourself. Ask about their previous experiences. Make sure to get a really good feel for this person because they will be in your home providing substantial personal care for your loved one. Be sure they can give you a list of references. Only hire someone who seems professional, trained, and compassionate.

Once you select a homecare assistant, make sure you're on the same page. Write a list of all the caregiving responsibilities you would like them to do. This might include personal care activities such as bathing, toileting, and feeding. It may also include recording medications and any other logs you keep. Many home-health aides and assistants may have hospice experience. However, some may not. Therefore, I encourage you to review the list and ask if they need to be shown anything in particular or have any questions. All in all, make sure you and your loved one feel comfortable with your homecare assistant.

TIP #47
WHEN IN DOUBT, ALERT YOUR CARE TEAM

"Our lives are stories in which we write, direct and star in the leading role. Some chapters are happy while others bring lessons to learn, but we always have the power to be the heroes of our own adventures."

- Joelle Speranza

WHEN IN DOUBT, call your healthcare or hospice team. If something seems to be going wrong, if something doesn't feel right, or if there appears to be a change in your loved one's condition, let your healthcare team know. While the change may be an expected part of the disease process, it's always helpful to check in with your care team in case a new care plan is needed to keep your loved one comfortable. Communicating with your healthcare team will also make you feel more comfortable and confident in the care you provide. So ease your mind - call.

Tip #48
Keep One Small Promise To Yourself

"Find out who you are and be that person. That's what your soul was put on this Earth to be. Find that truth, live that truth, and everything else will come."

- Ellen DeGeneres

MAKE A PROMISE TO YOURSELF, big or small, and keep it for the next seven days. When those seven days are up, make a new promise to yourself for the next seven days while doing your best to maintain the previous commitment. Keep this going.

By continuing this process, you are doing two important things. First, you are learning to trust yourself. Having the ability to trust in yourself is incredibly powerful. It builds self-confidence and self-esteem, leading to more positive life experiences and relationships. Second, you are rewiring your brain by creating new habits. Everything we are is a reflection of our daily habits. Our mood, our health, our relationships, our weight, our wealth, our mindset, our current life, our future life – they are all dependent on your habits. You have the ability to consistently choose new actions, build new habits, and, in turn, transform your life.

If you don't know where to start, here are a few examples.

STRATEGY #1

- I promise to get up ten minutes earlier every day to create space for myself to be with my thoughts.
- I promise to eat something every morning, even if it's small.
- I promise to take a walk outside the house every day, even if it is short.
- I promise to talk to someone (friend, relative, therapist) about my feelings at least once weekly.
- I promise to get in bed before 11 p.m. every night, even if I do not fall asleep.

TIP #49
SET UP BOUNDARIES

"Love yourself enough to set boundaries. Your time and energy are precious and you get to decide how you use them. You teach people how to treat you by deciding what you will and won't accept."

- Anna Taylor

CARING FOR MY GRANDDAD, I constantly felt pulled to sleep over despite hiring an overnight caregiver to watch over him. Sleeping on a blowup mattress, I'd get very little sleep. Then, early the following morning, I'd drive over an hour to work and be back that evening to do it all over again. Slowly but surely, my energy dwindled, and my mood dropped. I couldn't keep doing this, or I'd lose it altogether.

That's when I learned about boundaries. I needed to find a way to protect my sleep and my space. From then on, I relentlessly stuck by my newest boundary: sleep in my bed every night, no questions asked. There was no guilt to hold onto since owning my needs meant showing up with brighter energy for myself and those around me.

Now it's your time.

Most of us know what the word boundary means, but don't fully understand its concept. Boundaries can take many forms and look different for everyone. They can also change depending on where we are in our lives. Boundaries are the ground rules and limits you create to establish what you feel comfortable and safe with when interacting with others. They tell you and other people what behaviors, interactions, and communications you will tolerate and what you will not. Just like a "Do Not Enter" sign tells you not to go any farther, boundaries give you and those you engage with distinct borders of what is acceptable to you.

Your boundaries are set up based on the amount of physical and emotional capacity you have for others. Think about how much space you need for yourself and how much energy you can manage from others. Your boundaries are critical for maintaining our physical, mental, and emotional health and well-being. Because boundaries are invisible to everyone but yourself, it is essential to communicate the guidelines you've established with others. It is even more crucial to verbalize when these lines have been crossed.

Here are some examples of some critical boundaries to think about during this time.

STRATEGY #1

- I will limit the number of people I update and communicate with about my dying loved one's status to one person once a week.
- I will limit the number of visitors to the house to three people per week for no more than one hour each visit.
- I will put my phone on "silent" mode and only check text messages and voicemails when I have the energy. This does not have to be today.

- I will not allow myself to stay inside for more than 24 hours.
- Because I know _____ brings my energy down, I will spend no more than 15 minutes with them at a time.
- Create a list of specific things or topics you do not want others to say or talk about in your presence. In other words, these phrases, terms, or issues are off-limits to discuss with you.

Setting up and maintaining your boundaries will lead to a happier you and healthier relationships with others.

TIP #50
FORGIVE YOURSELF

"Forgive yourself, you are not perfect. Show yourself grace; you are still learning. Show yourself patience; you are on a journey."

- Shannon Yvette Tanner

FORGIVENESS IS A CHOICE.

For me, it has always been much harder to forgive myself than it is to forgive other people. But I've realized that holding on to that shame, guilt, blame, anger, sadness, or any other feeling for a mistake you made only causes more harm. We all make mistakes. We're human. It's a part of life. Learn from them, forgive yourself, and move on. *Free* yourself from the negative feelings you are clinging to by showing yourself compassion, love, and grace. Think about how much lighter you will feel.

Now, move forward in peace.

Tip #51

Forgive Others

"Forgiveness is for yourself because it frees you. It lets you out of that prison you put yourself in."

- Louise Hay

Forgiving someone is not for them; it's for you.

For some, this can take time, effort, and sometimes an outsider to help you work through the pain, trauma, or harm caused. Choosing to hold onto pain only hurts you more, mentally and physically. Allow yourself time to process and understand what happened and how it affected you without judgment. Decide to forgive them and set yourself free. Forgiving is healing. Feel the lightness of peace in your body, mind, and soul.

TIP #52
GET INTO NATURE

"Nature is not a place to visit. It is home."

- Gary Snyder

STEP outside the home where you are providing care at least once daily. It's easy to get trapped in this new caregiving role, and before you know it, it's been days since you've had a breath of fresh air. There are considerable advantages to being in nature, from lowering stress and soothing the mind to improving physical health and quality of life.

When caring for my Granddad, I would go days without leaving his house. I didn't realize how caught up I was in the caregiver mentality – never thinking about myself or my own needs. Finally, after several days, I was forced out of the house to return to work. Stepping outside and into my car, I noticed I immediately felt some weight lifted from my chest. I realized how long it had been since I'd been out for some fresh outdoor air. The longer I was away from the house and my care-giver mentality, the more I recognized how easy it was to get stuck in it without even knowing.

There happened to be a small wooded area just a short walk away from my Grandparents' home. So from that point on, when things were quiet and settled, I would make an effort to step outside the house and make my way through the trees for a short walk every afternoon. It was a wonderfully freeing feeling to look up at the trees and sky, to have some separation from caregiving, and to clear my mind.

So get yourself outside. It's good for you! Take a slow deep breath and fill your lungs with fresh, Earthly air. Smell the trees, plants, or flow-ers. See what happens when you look up at the sky. Watch the clouds move above you. Feel the breeze on your skin.Watch the birds fly around you. Find yourself at the edge of a stream, in a park, or surrounded by Earth's natural beauty. And feel some of the pressure inside you release into the air all around you.

TIP #53
LET GO OF WHAT IS OUT OF YOUR CONTROL

"Let go of certainty. The opposite isn't uncertainty. It's openness, curiosity and a willingness to embrace paradox, rather than choose up sides. The ultimate challenge is to accept ourselves exactly as we are, but never stop trying to learn and grow."

- Tony Schwartz

A HARD TRUTH TO LIFE: There are always things in life that we cannot control. For most of us, it's a hard pill to swallow.

Why is it so scary to give up control?

To control is to know. As humans, we like "knowns." It makes us feel safe and secure. It gives us a sense of certainty. On the other hand, the unknown makes us feel uncomfortable. It causes us to worry about the future because it's unpredictable and obscure.

It's a fact of life that you cannot control anything outside of yourself, and it's simply wasting your energy thinking that you can. From traffic, weather, and your aging body to the passing of time, the past, and other people's actions or feelings.

As a caregiver, you overthink because you care. You don't want to let anyone down. You don't want to fail your loved one, yourself, or others. But, **Dear Caregiver**, no amount of worrying, over-analyzing, or even planning can give you control over the future - over what happens next. So loosen your grip.

Permit yourself to let go while holding onto trust and faith in all that will be. By doing so, you free yourself from the source of pain and suffering that has been holding you down. Breathe. Let go. Move forward and allow yourself to experience life as it comes.

STRATEGY #1

To practice letting go, evaluate your need to control your situation:

- Why do you want to have control?
- What worries you about letting go of control?
- What would happen if you allowed yourself to let go of trying to have control?
- What is trying to control the uncontrollable doing for yourself and others?
- What would it feel like to let go of what is out of your control?
- What would it feel like to trust the journey?
- What are the benefits of letting go of what is out of my control?

STRATEGY #2

Things to let go of...

- "Mustakes" (Mistakes you must make to learn and grow.)
- Saying yes to everything
- The need to always be right
- Worrying about what others think or feel
- Constant blaming
- Constant complaining
- Guilt and anger about the past
- Fear of change
- Unrealistic expectations
- Controlling other people's behaviors
- Trying to please everyone

Tip #54
Put Effort Into What You Can Control

"Don't worry about what you can't control. Our focus and energy need to be on the things we can control. Attitude, effort, focus – these are the things we can control... "

- Tim Tebow

WHEN LIFE SEEMS WILDLY OUT of control, there is always something within the chaos that can help you reclaim your sense of order. While Tip #53 reminds us that you can't control anything around you, you can focus on your response, attitude, behaviors, and reactions. Placing your effort, energy, and actions into what you can control empowers you to move past the victim mentality and further step into a more powerful you.

STRATEGY #1

Write down a list of everything you have control over in your life. Notice these things only relate to yourself.

- Pay attention to your everyday thoughts, feelings, reactions, attitudes, moods, behaviors, patterns, and habits.
- Think about how you want your life to look. What does your ideal life look like? Who are you, and how are you showing up in the world? What does your ideal Self feel like?
- Are your current thoughts, feelings, reactions, attitudes, moods, behaviors, patterns, and habits helping or hindering your ideal life and ideal Self?
- What is one thing you can do or change within your control to get one small step closer to your ideal life and Self?

TIP #55
DON'T GET DOWN ON YOURSELF

"Don't be a victim of negative self-talk. Remember, you are listening."

- Bob Proctor

DOESN'T it feel good when you say something positive to yourself? Similarly, doesn't it make you feel terrible when you say something negative to yourself? What we tell ourselves is what we become. In other words, we are what we tell ourselves.

What have you been telling yourself lately?

It's common for caregivers to put themselves down for one reason or another. You might feel like you're not doing a "good enough" job. You might feel like it's your fault that your loved one is in this position. You might feel like you aren't doing this "caregiving thing" right. It's easy to feel discouraged, but you've got to stop bullying yourself. You'd never let your friend speak to themselves like this. Nor would you say these negative things to them. Know that this is your inner critic trying to get the best of you. Don't let it get one over on you. You have the power to talk back.

Stop dwelling on your mistakes, failures, and missteps. Stop second-guessing the things you should or should not have done or things you should or should not have said. We're all here just trying to do our best, and *that* is what matters! We keep learning, and we keep growing. That's the amazing thing about life.

We all have self-critical thoughts. It takes emotional maturity to respond rather than react to them. The less you pay attention to your inner critic, the quieter it becomes. Remember, negative thoughts will pass. Focusing on the positive will shift your current perspective and help your self-critical thoughts move on. It takes courage to talk back with positivity. Yet, by doing so, you become a stronger version of yourself and an even better caregiver.

These are the red flag words to look out for…

"I should"
"I shouldn't"
"I can't"
"I'm too… "

If you hear these words, chances are your inner critic is trying to knock you down. Use the strategies below to knock it back.

STRATEGY #1

When your inner critic needs to back off, try these steps.

STEP 1
Notice any negative thoughts that are popping up.

STEP 2
Accept that you are doing the best you can and allow the thought

replaying in your mind to fade. Remember, thoughts always come and go, and this, too, shall pass.

STEP 3
Challenge the thought you are having. Is this thought helping or hurting you? Is it valid? Is it fact? What advice would you give a friend if they had this same thought?

STEP 4
Use positive affirmations to rewrite your script. (See Tip #39)

This negative self-talk doesn't change anything and only damages your self-esteem, self-worth, and self-confidence.

STRATEGY #2

Embrace self-compassion by replacing negative self-talk spirals with positive ones.

For example, replace:

- "I can't believe I did _____!" with "Next time I can be better by doing _____."
- "I'm not good enough." with "I am enough and I am continuing to work on my progress."
- "I shouldn't have said _____." with "This is a great opportunity to learn from. I am learning more and more everyday."

TIP #56

LEARN FROM YOUR MISTAKES

"I haven't failed. I've just found 10,000 ways that won't work."

- Thomas Edison

THE FIRST TIME I tried to clean the soiled diaper of an adult, change their clothes, move them from their bed to a chair, and position them comfortably, oh boy, it was a sight to see. I was a mess. They were a mess. It was a total disaster. The only thing I could do was try better next time.

Let's face it; you are not going to get everything right. You are not going to be perfect. You are going to make mistakes. And that's okay. In fact, expect mistakes. Mistakes are good. Every mistake is an opportunity to learn, grow, and evolve. Rather than condemn your supposed "failures," reframe them as life's little lessons.

Strategy #1

Ask yourself these questions…

- What went wrong?
- What did I learn?
- How can I make it better next time?

Now get back on the horse and try again.

You got this.

TIP #57
BE PRESENT, IT'S TRULY A PRESENT

"If you are depressed you are living in the past.
If you are anxious you are living in the future.
If you are at peace you are living in the present."

- Lao Tzu

TO "RUMINATE" means to reflect repeatedly on an idea or decision, past, present, or future. We obsessively replay a thought over and over despite desperately wanting to stop. It's like an unwelcome guest in our minds. As a caregiver, dwelling on past events, mistakes, and negative feelings are common. Similarly, worrying about the future is common, often creating catastrophes in our minds. These thoughts can be debilitating.

Spending too much time agonizing over the past and future leads to depression, anxiety, and chronic pain. It is impossible to go back in time; however, there is always an opportunity to learn from it. Likewise, it is impossible to be one hundred percent certain of the future, but we can try our best to plan for it.

Wasting time and energy stewing over things that are impossible to change or control removes you from the present. Remember, the only thing we ever have is the present moment. It's the only place we can truly be, and that is what makes it so precious. If you don't slow down and can't be where you are, you will miss your life. You will miss the time you have with your loved one. In the grand scheme of life, we are only here for a limited time.

So, be here *now*.

Practice being present when you are alone, with others, and with the loved one you are caring for. In many ways, this relates to Tip #34.

STRATEGY #1

When you are alone, create moments of silence throughout your day. You might find this quiet time in a private room or outside. You might find it in the bathroom or before bed. In these delicate moments, practice the strategies discussed in Tips #33 and #34.

Silencing external noise allows your nervous system to relax and find a restorative state. Your mind can refocus on the here and now from this invaluable space. What can you be grateful for at this moment?

STRATEGY #2

When you are with others, create moments of pause. A simple pause gives you power over your mind. It gives you the chance to become aware of your thoughts, feelings, and reactions. While typically habitual and learned, self-awareness builds opportunities to be more intentional.

For example, your sibling comes over to visit for the first time this month. They ridicule your caregiving ways and are convinced "their ways" are better.

- How would you feel?
- How would you react?

Take some time to think about this.

- What if, before reacting, you use the power of a pause?

To do this, count backward from ten to interrupt your initial thought and stop your habitual reaction. In this countdown, you get the opportunity to decide whether this thought and reaction are helpful or hurtful. Pausing gives you immediate control and allows you to choose a more productive response.

A pause allows you to stop and evaluate – to question the reality and rationality of your perceptions and actions in the present moment. You have the opportunity to rethink and choose differently – a different feeling, response, or behavior. You always have the freedom and power of choice. Instead of allowing your initial thoughts and gut reactions to take over, be in the moment. Make a decision that aligns with you.

STRATEGY #3

One of the most important things you can do when caring for your loved one is to be present - be in the Now.

Be intentional about creating quality time that allows you to bond, connect, and grow closer.

Talk with them.

Smile with them.

Laugh with them.

Cry with them.

Just be there with them, by their side. They won't be here forever, and you cannot get these moments back. So don't miss it.

Say all the things. Do all the things. Be grateful for every moment you have with them.

STRATEGY #4

For obsessive thoughts about the past, consider these questions.

- Is the worry accurate and rational, or could it be inaccurate or an overreaction?
- Is this worry helping me (and others) or hurting me (and others)?
- Is there something you can do about this now?
- Is there something you can do to fix this later?
- If not, what have you learned?
- What are the steps to prevent this from happening next time?

STRATEGY #5

Consider these questions if you find yourself worrying or catastrophizing an event in the future

- Is your worry valid or an overreaction?
- Is this worry helping me (and others) or hurting me (and others)?
- How likely is it that your concern or fear will actually happen?

- What steps or actions can you take to prevent this worry from occurring?
- What steps and actions can you take to create a better outcome?

TIP #58
WHEN THINGS GET HARD... KEEP GOING!

"If you're going through hell... keep going."

- Winston Churchill

...BECAUSE YOU WOULDN'T STOP in hell, would you? Every difficult situation I experience becomes my greatest teacher. Every breakdown becomes a catalyst for a breakthrough. These moments are always a gift and the chance to gain a lesson, skill, person, or experience. Knowing this gives me faith. It is the anchor that grounds me. It is the power that moves me through every challenge, obstacle, and awful moment that comes my way. I know that this moment, as terrible as it may be, is preparing me for something that hasn't yet happened. And so, I keep going.

There are times in our lives when the only thing we can do is keep going. You must simply put one foot in front of the other. Take every day One. Day. At. A. Time. And take every moment One. Moment. At. A. Time. I know things are really hard. It seems like you're stuck with no ending in sight. You're barely standing with two feet on the ground. In the moments you think you can't, keep going anyway. Repeat the affirmation, "Yes I can."

It is through our challenges, obstacles, and hardships that we build resilience. Right now, you are discovering your true strength. Please remember, this is not your forever. Have faith something is waiting for you on the other side. Your future self will thank you for not giving up.

I hope one day you look back on this time and never forget that when things were tough, when you were exhausted and overwhelmed, when you felt isolated and alone, when you didn't have the answers and couldn't see through the fog, when you wanted to surrender and give up, you kept going.

STRATEGY #1

Repeat one or several of these phrases to yourself.

- "I am safe."
- "I'm okay."
- "I can do this."
- "I've made it through so many hard things before this. I will make it through this, too."
- "This moment is meant for me. It will all be clear to me later."

STRATEGY #2

Focus on the small picture, not the big picture. Break everything down into bite size steps or moments. Remind yourself you only have to get through this day, rather than the next 12 months. Ask yourself...

"What can I do to help me get through the next hour?"

Once you are through this moment, focus on getting through the next.

The big picture is scary and overwhelming. But, when you break it down into mini parts, each situation, incident, and circumstance feels manageable.

STRATEGY #3

Remember to breathe, just breathe.

Breathe in slowly. Hold for a second. Now, let it go slowly. Repeat.

Refer to Tip #35 for breathing exercises.

TIP #59
RESPECT OUR DIFFERENCES

"Tolerance implies a respect for another person, not because he is wrong or even because he is right, but because he is human."

- John Cogley

YOU WILL NOT ALWAYS AGREE with your family. You will not always agree with your healthcare or hospice team. You will not always agree with your dying loved one. We all see the world through our own eyes and no one else's. You will never be able to experience the world from someone else's shoes.

You may look at a situation and think one way, while someone else may look at the same situation and, for whatever reason, think something totally different. Knowing everyone's emotions are running high, seek to understand their point of view rather than let your differences create anger. Even if you disagree, understand everyone has and is allowed to have their perspective.

STRATEGY #1

"I" STATEMENTS

Always use "I" statements to confront others or express your needs and feelings.

For example…

- I feel worried when…
- I feel hurt because…
- I feel upset when…
- I think that I…
- When I think I'm not being appreciated I…
- When I'm told I'm doing something wrong I…
- I get really anxious when…
- I would like...

STRATEGY #2

Be curious.
Ask questions.
Listen intently.
Don't assume.
Seek to understand.
Validate their feelings.
Be self-reflective.

TIP #60
DIVVY UP THE RESPONSIBILITIES

"Alone, we can do so little; together, we can do so much."

- Helen Keller

YOU MIGHT NOTICE we've touched on this here and there throughout this book. However, this time, we will address this situation with specific suggestions.

You are only one person and can only do so much alone. Do what you can to split up the many caregiving responsibilities related to caring and preparing for your loved one's needs.

STRATEGY #1

For example, divide and conquer responsibilities among family members , relatives, or other closely connected friends.

- Give someone the responsibility of handling your loved one's finances.
- Give someone the responsibility of communicating with other friends, family, relatives, and healthcare professionals.
- Give someone the responsibility of seeking out funeral home options and possible arrangements if your loved one is dying or nearing the end of their life.
- Give someone the responsibility of searching for and seeking out additional homecare assistance.
- Give someone the responsibility of caring for your loved one on the weekends or a specific day of the week so you can rest.
- Give someone the responsibility of doing the food shopping and ordering of caregiving supplies.
- Give someone the responsibility of estate planning duties.

TIP #61
LOOKIN' FANCY

"Fashion is the armor to survive the reality of everyday life."

- Bill Cunningham

MORE OFTEN THAN NOT, you're likely finding yourself in your "comfy clothes" these days. It's easy to fall into this habit when you're inside most of the day caring for your loved one. You think, "Well I'm not going out anywhere. I'm not going to see anyone. Plus, I'm tired and this is more comfortable."

In Tip #6, we remember how it feels to put on clean clothes daily. Nothing makes us feel fresher and more ready for a new day like clean clothes on our backs. But here, I want you to remember what it feels like to get ready for an extra special night.

You shower. You shave. You rub lotion on your skin. You wear deodorant. You trim your nails, maybe paint them. You do up your hair. You put on fancy clothes. You slide into nice shoes. Perhaps you do your make-up and put on jewelry. Or you strap a nice watch to your wrist. You spray yourself with cologne or perfume. Finally, you turn to look at yourself in the mirror, and *wow*.

"Dang! I look good," you think to yourself.

And that makes you feel *extra* special. You deserve to feel good in your skin again. And I mean, *really* good. Even if it's just for you. Even if you aren't *going* anywhere.

Do it for *YOU*.

TIP #62
TREAT YOURSELF

"Self-compassion is simply giving the same kindness to ourselves that we would give to others."

- Christopher Germer

WHILE THIS TIP will vary depending on your financial situation, use this tip to remind yourself you are worthy and deserving. You are working so hard. You are doing such a good job. You are selflessly giving your time and energy to help someone you love, maybe even seeing them through to the end of their life's journey. You deserve to treat yourself to something that makes you feel spectacular and abundant.

STRATEGY #1

Here are just a few ideas…

- Get your nails done.
- Get a body massage.
- Get a facial or skin care treatment.
- Go to a restaurant, winery, or brewery and order an interesting, fun, or exciting drink or food item.
- See a movie at the theater and enjoy your favorite movie snack.

If finances are tight, here are some other money-saving self-love ideas...

- Do your own nails. Find fun and inexpensive nail polish that excites you. Pour some hot water into a small bowl with soap, resting your fingers in it for a few minutes. Clip and file your nails before painting on your new polish.
- Find an inexpensive hand-held massage tool or back scratcher and use it on all the muscles you can reach.
- Sit in a hot bubble bath. Add bath salts. Dim the lights. Light candles around you. Turn on your favorite music.
- Create a new and intriguing cocktail, mocktail, or food item from whatever you have in the kitchen. Use Google or an app like Pinterest to search for recipes.
- Have a movie night at home and set the scene: Lights turned off, feet up on a footrest, and popcorn in hand.

TIP #63
LAUGH OFTEN

"Laughter is the lubricant that makes life liveable."

- Russell Howard

I WORKED with a family whose father, Bill, was dying. Bill's wife, children, and grandchildren surrounded his bed every minute of every day. There were a lot of tears, sad faces, and hearts that were breaking. The distressing energy was palpable as I walked into their home. As Bill became unresponsive, his family kept waiting at his bedside, wondering when he would die. But Bill kept on going, lying in bed, silent and still.

Finally, one evening, Bill's family gathered in the kitchen for a brief while. Someone shared a story that made Bill's wife and entire family laugh uncontrollably. Then, just for a moment, the energy shifted. Soon after, Bill's wife walked back into his room and found Bill had finally died. It was as if his family's laughter was the seal of approval he was waiting for.

Truthfully, laughter is like magic. It can make something that feels so terrible or stressful seem *lighter*. It is one of the best-known cures for stress and sadness. You know that feeling when something is going so wrong that you either laugh or cry? Laughter makes the experience feel less awful, almost funny. Whenever you can, try to find humor in your day. Because laughter is the remedy. The antidote. The key to sanity.

Laughter is universal. It is contagious. It binds us together, fills us with joy, and creates beautiful memories in our souls. So find a way to laugh at the good, bad, and ugly.

STRATEGY #1

Play this laughing game with your loved one (or anyone else in your home).

First, flip a coin to decide who will go first.

Next, each person will take turns faking a laugh for ten seconds.

The object of the game is to be the first person to make the other person laugh using their fake one.

Continue to swap turns until there is a winner.

Don't be surprised if you both end up on the floor laughing hysterically with one another.

STRATEGY #2

Search for "funny animal memes" online.

STRATEGY #3

Watch or listen to a comedian of your choice.

STRATEGY #4

Most of us have someone in our lives who always has a way of making us laugh. Think about who this person is in your life and invite them to visit.

TIP #64
BE FLEXIBLE

"The oak is the strongest tree in the forest, but the willow bends and adapts. When the fires and storms hit, it is the willow that survives."

- Kara Barbieri

LIFE IS NOT ALWAYS GOING to go as planned. Things happen. Life happens. Most of those things are out of anyone's control. Other times, plans change. Either way, adapt and allow for flexibility. Let go of expectations because, let's be honest, caregiving never goes as expected. Be willing to go with the flow. Energy spent on worrying, stressing, or getting upset is energy wasted. It's okay to be disappointed, but be willing to move forward.

STRATEGY #1

- *Your nurse is stuck at another patient's emergency and can't get to yours immediately.*

Try to talk through your situation on the phone with another hospice nurse or ask if another nurse is available to come out sooner.

- *Your aide is sick, and all the other hospice aides' schedules are busy.*

Ask a relative, friend, or neighbor to help you wash, change, and reposition your loved one. AND request that your hospice provide an additional day of aide support to make up for the lost day.

- *Your sister has no one to pick up her child from soccer practice and take him to his doctor's appointment. So she now has to reschedule her visit with Mom, which was supposed to give you a break from caregiving today.*

Ask your sister to relieve you tomorrow instead. Ask a neighbor or close friend if they are available for an hour so you can step out for a little break.

- *Your brother hasn't seen Dad in over a year and is on his way to see him before he dies. But, unfortunately, dad takes his last breath before your brother arrives.*

Hug and comfort your brother when he arrives. Reinforce that Dad loved him and knew how much he loved Dad. But Dad couldn't wait. It was his time.

These are only a few of the many potential scenarios. The important thing is to know change is inevitable. During any day in everyone's life, caregiver or not, things are going to happen that no one would be able to see coming – right out of the blue. There are no emotions tied to these events. You get to decide how to react and the feeling to attach. Avoid falling into the constant trap of cursing the unpredictable.

Being flexible allows you to adjust and adapt to unexpected changes easily. The result? Lowered stress. It will keep you grounded in the present moment.

TIP #65
THE POWER OF A HUG

"You yourself, as much as anybody in the entire universe, deserve your love and affection."

- Buddha

A PERSONAL STORY: When the COVID-19 pandemic shut our world down in 2020, I went more than 60 days without physical touch from another human being. I had been noticing more and more that something was going on with me, but I couldn't quite pinpoint it. I was feeling more and more rotten by the day.

One evening I was on a zoom call with my family when I suddenly noticed every other person in my family touching the significant other sitting next to them. And I realized I was the only one who wasn't. That's when it hit me. I was craving human contact and human touch. A rush of emotion hit me as I sat in the shower, sobbing my eyes out. What I needed was a hug. So I returned to my room and wrapped my arms around myself. I hugged myself. The longer I held on, the more my body softened. Finally, I remembered what it was like to be hugged, even if it was a hug from myself.

Hugs are valuable because they activate the emotional processing center in our brains through different nerve pathways. They release neurochemicals and hormones, such as oxytocin and endorphins, which make us feel good. Oxytocin is the soothing hormone. It makes us feel loved, trusted, and bonded to others. It also helps to slow the heart rate, decrease stress, and lower anxiety. The brain's reward system also releases endorphins, which give us feelings of comfort, safety, and wholeness. A hug may also help improve your sleep and even help boost your immune system.

STRATEGY #1

Whether hugging yourself like I did or hugging those around you, take time for a hug. The longer you hold on, the more you activate these feel-good hormones.

Tip #66

Detox

"Things changed when my phone outsmarted me. Once Facebook had a permanent place in my pocket, it became a permanent portal—able to transport me away from my family. Even if we were physically in the same room, I wasn't necessarily there with them. Facebook was no longer simply a naptime vacation but an all-day form of escapism."

- Wendy Speake

FIRST THING IN THE MORNING, what do you do? Before moving on, really think about this question.

You likely turn off the alarm you set on your smartphone, then quickly check for text messages that may have appeared overnight. While grabbing coffee and breakfast, you watch, listen to, or read the morning news on your phone or T.V. while scrolling through Facebook (now called Meta), Instagram, TikTok, or Twitter. You check emails, chat through texts, and google-search your latest caregiver question throughout the day. Finally, after a tiring day of caring for your loved one, you crash on the couch binging Netflix while, yet again, plugging into the latest photos your friends (or acquaintances) have posted on social media. This is a typical way of life today.

In 2020, estimates show the average American spent approximately 1,300 hours on social media. That's about three and a half hours per day. With more social, shopping, and lifestyle apps appearing daily, that number has likely only increased.

It's hard, tapping on Facebook and instantly seeing how amazing everyone's life is but yours. An old high school acquaintance, who, by the way, you haven't spoken to in over 30 years, just bought a boat and sailed the Caribbean. Your best friend's daughter just got married and is relaxing on the Greek islands with her new husband. Your brother-in-law's parents are glowing as they celebrate their 60th wedding anniversary.

You scroll, and you scroll, getting sucked in one post after the next. Soon you've wasted an hour looking at "how great people's lives must be," feeling even worse than before you unlocked your phone. You were just trying to order adult briefs on Amazon. How did you even get here?

We are so plugged into the outside world that we lose the most important thing we have – the here and now. Social media does this to us. It sucks us in as it drowns out everything that is our current life today. The news scares or angers us. Instagram gives us "FOMO," or Fear Of Missing Out. Facebook (Meta) makes us feel isolated as we compare ourselves to the "incredible" lives of others. TikTok numbs our feelings. Twitter leaves us feeling bullied or ashamed.

What does all social media have in common? It makes us feel worse about ourselves and our own lives or situations. Don't get me wrong; technology is a wonderful tool with many benefits. We have information at our fingertips and the ability to stay connected with those we love worldwide. However, taking a digital detox and cutting back on screen time, especially when it's been wreaking silent havoc on your life, can bring you back to living in the moment and at your best. I've done it, so I can attest.

If you've been feeling depressed, isolated, irritable, insecure, frustrated, or finding yourself consumed by social media notifications, it's time to *unplug*. Using these strategies, give yourself a break from screens, social apps, and television.

STRATEGY #1

This is the strategy I like to use whenever I need a digital detox.

STEP 1
Place your phone in constant "silent" mode. Yes, that means 24 hours a day.

STEP 2
Delete the social media applications you tend to get lost in more often than not. For me, this includes Instagram and Facebook (Meta). Make sure they delete these apps from your smartphone and any other device you use.

STEP 3
Intentionally set goals for yourself to maintain this detox.

For example...

- Do not look at your phone – other than turning off the alarm – for at least one hour after waking up in the morning.
- Do not look at your phone – other than setting your alarm – for at least 30 minutes before bed.
- Set up specific times of the day that you will allow yourself to use your phone to check text messages, phone calls, or emails. I recommend allowing yourself one to three times per day. *In an emergency, this rule does not apply.*
- Decide how long your digital detox will continue, and mark this date on your calendar. Then, choose to commit to this

goal daily. For example, I digitally detox for one week every month.

STRATEGY #2

Use the following questions to develop a plan to help you unplug from screens and technology.

- What is the biggest issue for you when it comes to the digital world?
- What behavior do you want to change, and what activities do you want to decrease?

For example, do you spend too much time on your smartphone? Are attached to or spend too much time on certain social media apps? Does the news add to your stress?

- What goal do you want to set for yourself to decrease screen time?

For example, do you want to eliminate the use altogether? Will you limit the use to specific times of the day? Will you limit the use to set time frames such as 15 minutes? How long will this detox last – Every Sunday? Seven days? Two weeks? One month?

- What will help you stay committed to this goal?

For example, will you need to delete applications? Will you need to keep your devices in a spare room? Will you need to turn your phone off? Will you need support from family or friends?

Be sure to check in with yourself after a few days of your detox. How are you feeling?

Be proud of your progress. Have faith in yourself. You can do this.

STRATEGY #3

In addition to social media, you may need to detox from certain people. Think about all the different people you interact with or surround yourself with in your life.

We all have people in our lives who light us up and who make us feel happy and good. These are the people you want to create more space for.

We also know people in our lives who drain us or make us feel anxious and low. Consider who these people might be for you and create more distance and space between your interactions.

How do you know who these people are? Consider these questions.

- Who do you interact with who is always negative?
- Who in your life tends to drag you down when you spend time with them?
- Who makes you feel tense, stressed, or insecure when you are around them?
- Who sucks the energy right out of you, leaving you ready for alone time?

Helpful Hint

If you are using social media as a support system, consider setting specific boundaries for yourself. For example, if you are a part of our online Death.Care.Coach Community Support Group on Facebook (Meta), limit your use of Facebook to this group and nothing else.

TIP #67
SEXY TIME

"Sex is a natural thing – it is physical, it is there in the body. But sexuality is invented and created by you."

- Sadhguru

LET'S TALK ABOUT SEX.

Yes, you read that right. Studies have found sex is not only beneficial for our health and boosts our overall well-being. Benefits range from strengthening the immune system, lowering blood pressure, and improving the health of your heart to decreasing stress, depression, and anxiety, boosting self-esteem, and improving your sleep. Sex also acts as an immediate natural pain reliever. In relationships, it can also enhance intimacy and connection with your partner.

In a 2021 study, researchers observed the mental wellness of males and females of all ages throughout the COVID-19 pandemic. The study discovered sexual function had a direct impact on psychological well-being. Those partaking in sexual activity reported improved mental health, as well as improved interpersonal connections. Additionally, the study found those who were less sexually active experienced more psychological distress, such as depression and anxiety, and were less likely to maintain spousal or partner relationships. And while both sexes were affected, females had an increased risk for depression and anxiety compared to males.

Sex stimulates and activates different hormones and chemicals within our bodies, including endorphins, dopamine, and serotonin. In addition, when intimate with our partner, we also produce oxytocin, a hormone known as the "love drug." All four hormones are known to make us feel good and boost our overall well-being.

Sex is complex yet a central aspect of being human. Everyone has personal preferences, beliefs, and comfort levels regarding sex and sexual activity. That makes us all unique, and therefore will each approach this tip in our own way. This tip is not meant to be offensive or abrasive. Rather, it is to open your mind to the possibility that having sex or partaking in another form of sexual activity may help relieve stress and make you feel better.

As a caregiver, it might be tough to find the energy to even think about sex. The chronic demands of caregiving are wearing and may even decrease your libido (your sex drive). However, when it comes to sex drive, it's been shown that having more sex boosts your libido.

So, how might this look for you, whether you have a partner or not? How might you reasonably honor this part of you? I'll leave you to develop your own strategies as this will look different for all of us.

TIP #68
I BELIEVE

"To have faith is to trust yourself to the water. When you swim you don't grab hold of the water, because if you do you will sink and drown. Instead you relax, and float."

- Alan W. Watts

WHEN YOU'RE LOST and struggling to find your way, keep your faith. Sometimes that's all we have. In many ways this relates to Tip #58. No one knows what the future holds, but you have to trust. Trust that everything is going to be okay. Trust that what is meant for you will find you. Trust that while the journey is grueling, the view from the top of the mountain is spectacular.

Have faith that there is purpose and meaning to this. While it might be impossible to know now, trust that the answers will come to you at a later date. Believe in yourself. Believe in your ability. *Faith* keeps you going.

"How is it possible to trust and have faith at at time like this?" You ask. Think about a time in your life that challenged you. How did you get through it? What came out of that experience? Looking back, how did it change you? How did it help you grow? What is one positive thing that came out of that difficult moment? Remember, time will give you a new perspective, so keep believing.

STRATEGY #1

Repeat these words to yourself before getting out of bed every morning.

"I believe. I believe. I believe."

STRATEGY #2

If it feels right, pray.

Pray to your God or Gods.
Pray to the Universe.
Pray to Source Energy.
Pray to everyone or no one.

STRATEGY #3

Reach out to your support network

- Family
- Friends
- Community
- Accountability Partner
- Therapist or Counselor
- Healthcare Team
- Spiritual Leaders or Members

STRATEGY #4

Envision your most ideal future self and life. Consider the steps and actions you will need to take in order to create this vision into your reality. Consider your fears. What is stopping you?

- Write down these steps. If you don't know all of the steps yet, write down the next action you can take.

Tip #69
Don't Wipe Away Those Tears

"Crying's always been a way for me to get things out which are buried deep, deep down. When I sing, I often cry. Crying is feeling, and feeling is being human."

- Ray Charles

SOMETIMES YOU JUST NEED A GOOD cry. Even if you have no idea what you're crying about.

For me, this happens at least a few times a year. Sometimes life just piles on top of you, load after load. If it's not this, it's that. If it's not that, it's this. I usually get to a point where I feel it. I feel the cry coming on like a sneeze tickling my nose. I know it's coming, tickle after tickle, but it waits for just the right moment. Then, often when I'm least expecting it – boom. A sob fest explosion.

Sometimes it happens in the privacy of my own home, where I can let out that ugly cry without any embarrassment. I'm thankful for those moments. Other times I find myself making rather alarming whale noises while blowing snot at anyone nearby. In those more public moments, it was someone who said or did something that sparked the cry out of me. In either situation, no matter what, I always feel better. The sneeze was sneezed; with it, I let go of all the pressure trapped inside.

Meltdown accomplished.

Let this tip be your permission to let those tears flow. Ugly cry it out. Sob. Have a meltdown. Whimper. Scream. Whatever does it for you. It's all okay. It's all good. Even science will support you. Crying releases natural feel-good chemicals such as oxytocin and body-producing opioids. So go ahead, sob your heart out and feel better for it.

TIP #70
SAY CHEESE

"You don't have to be happy to smile."

- Daniel Willey

SHIRLEY'S HUSBAND had a stroke that left him needing full-time care for the rest of his life. Shirley didn't get married expecting to be her husband's caregiver at 52 years old, but here she was. Learning the ins and outs of her husband's needs was challenging to say the least. He was paralyzed on the left side of his body with very little strength on his right side. He had difficulty speaking and swallowing. He was incontinent of urine and stool, which meant his briefs needed to be changed several times a day. He was also almost twice her size.

If you saw Shirley on the street or at the grocery store, you'd have no idea how much she dealt with every day. Walking into her home was just the same. Shirley had this constant smile on her face. It was the kind of smile that drew people in. The one that said, "Hey, everything's okay. Life is a gift, and I'm so excited I get to be here. Come and join me."

One day I asked Shirley how she kept her smile through it all. Her answer was simple. While she admitted there were times she had to fake it, getting through each day always felt better through a smile compared to a frown.

Have you ever passed someone with a big smile on their face, and it just made you smile back? Have you ever passed someone who wasn't smiling, but after eye contact and directing *your* smile towards them, it made them smile back? How did these interactions make you feel? You probably felt a little better, even for the slightest moment.

You've probably heard the saying, "It takes more muscles to frown than it does to smile." While I haven't found any sound evidence to support that statement, there are definite truths that back the benefits of a smile. When you smile, your brain releases tiny chemicals and hormones that work together to lower stress and boost your mood. Those feel-good hormones – endorphins, dopamine, and serotonin – are at it again, making us feel happier, calmer, and relieving our pain. And guess what? Seeing someone else smile activates the reward center in our brain, which only intensifies those feel-good effects.

Topping it off, if you've ever heard the other saying, "fake it 'til you make it," well, when it comes to smiling, there is some research to suggest you can still gain the same rewards by faking one. So, if you haven't smiled in a while, it's time to start. Here are some suggestions to help you turn that frown upside down.

STRATEGY #1

Upon waking up first thing in the morning, smile. You can even keep your eyes closed while lying in bed.

STRATEGY #2

While brushing your teeth every morning, look in the mirror and smile.

Be sure to make eye contact with yourself. You'll be giving and receiving a smile, sending those feel-good hormones through the roof.

STRATEGY #3

Ask your loved one to try a game with you.

Sit across from each other with a stopwatch or timer in hand. While making eye contact, see who can keep a smile the longest.

Don't be surprised if this ends up in laughter.

TIP #71
OPEN UP YOUR LENS

"What we see depends mainly on what we look for. ... In the same field, the farmer will notice the crop, the geologists the fossils, botanists the flowers, artists the coloring, sportsmen the cover for the game. Though we may all look at the same things, it does not all follow that we should see them."

- John Lubbock

YOU CAN ONLY SEE the world through your lens, never through anyone else's. Our lenses are all different colors, shades, shapes, and sizes. No one lens is the same. We each live in our own bodies, minds, and experiences. We all come from different backgrounds – families, cultures, socioeconomics, and education. Therefore, we are limited to our personal life experiences, which then mold our personal beliefs. These things affect how we see, understand, and interpret the world around us. This interpretation is our perspective. And our perspective is limited to the colors we, ourselves, have painted.

It's easy to get stuck viewing the world behind the same lens, especially under stress. As caregivers, we often land ourselves in tunnel vision. We think that our perspective is the objective truth. However, the reality is we all have our own truths, so it's necessary to consider that your opinion is not the only 'right way.'

It is possible to change your lens. You can open it up or change its position, but only if you are willing to try. Sometimes you need to take a step back to get a wider view. Sometimes you simply need to turn a little to the right or a little to the left. Either way, we end up with a new and often better vantage point. Similar to a camera lens, when you adjust the angle, you allow more into the frame, suddenly becoming aware of new ideas and new views that were there all along. These new reference points can help you reframe your current beliefs and, in turn, create a different outlook or attitude.

Here lies a new perspective.

Dear Caregiver,
Consider whether your lens may be stuck in a small frame.

Do you spend most of your time defending yourself? – What you say? What you do? What you believe?

Do you get angry or frustrated when someone doesn't agree with you or your opinion?

Do you firmly believe that someone else – your loved one, family member, or friend – is wrong?

If you answered "yes" to any of the questions above, challenge yourself with curiosity by exploring the strategies described in this tip. Remember, you are unaware of what you are unaware of. Ultimately, you can choose to zoom out. Changing your view just might change your life.

STRATEGY #1

Reframe your thoughts by replacing the words "I have to" with "I get to."

For example, instead of "I have to take care of them," try, "I get to take care of them."

Notice when swapping out these words, the connotation changes from negative to positive – an undesirable duty to a valuable opportunity.

This slight shift in perspective can lead to a drastic improvement in attitude and mindset.

STRATEGY #2

Change the angle of your viewpoint.

While it is impossible to see the world through anyone's eyes but our own, we can still try to adjust our perspective by listening and understanding the views of others. When you try to put yourself in their shoes, you may be able to empathize and appreciate a new perspective.

For example, you and your family might disagree with your loved one's care, making you both feel frustrated or angry.

In this example, you feel this way because you see the situation one way while they see it another. Using this strategy, ask your family questions to better understand what they believe to be true and where they are coming from.

Start with a non-judgmental phrase such as…

- I'd like to try to understand your view a little better. Would you mind if I asked some questions so I can try to recognize where you are coming from?

Follow up with questions that might include...

- What do you believe would be the best way to take care of them?
- Why is it important to you that they receive care in this way?
- What potential advantages and disadvantages might exist with your view of their care?
- What potential advantages and disadvantages do you see with my view of their care?
- Help me to understand why your opinion of their care might be more beneficial than my opinion of their care.
- How do you think [your loved one] would feel about your way of care? And what about my way of care?

STRATEGY #3

Try these steps when feeling overwhelmed, confused, or repeatedly looping back to a situation.

- Write down your perspective on the specific situation.
- Ask yourself, "What would it take to change my perspective?"
- Ask yourself, "Where did this perspective come from?" Then, consider the sources of your perspective, such as previous life experiences, family, friends, education, culture, and others.
- Ask yourself "What if" questions to help you envision what it would feel like if you decided to look at this situation differently.
- "What if I chose to be grateful for this situation?"

- "What if I chose to see more than one way of doing this?"
- "What if I chose to see this from their shoes?"
- "What if I chose to learn from this situation?
- "What if in ten years I look back and realize this situation taught me XYZ?"
- Ask yourself, "What new information can I learn or seek out to help me open my mind to new possibilities?"

CONCLUSION

"You can't go back and change the beginning, but you can start where you are and change the ending."

- C.S. Lewis

I don't think anyone ever imagines their life would lead them to become a caregiver, but here you are. Similarly, I don't think anyone imagines their life would lead them to become dependent and need to be taken care of, yet here is your loved one.

It is truly an incredible opportunity and an extraordinary gift to be with and care for a loved one in a time of need. And if this caregiving venture is the beginning of your loved one's end-of-life journey, that makes this time even more precious and meaningful. This is time you can't get back. Though it can be hard to see now, you will look back and value all these little moments with your loved one: the good, the bad, and even the ugly.

Despite how meaningful and valuable it is to be a caregiver, it is also a massive undertaking. The physical, mental, emotional, spiritual, social, financial, and occupational distress it can place on you, **Dear Caregiver**, is often overlooked and underappreciated. Many people have, will, and do struggle with recognizing, coping, and managing the chronic, ongoing stress that comes with caregiving.

Learning to take care of yourself when you have the responsibility of caring for your loved one and everything else in your life isn't easy. But doing so is vital.

Take a moment to imagine walking down a path and reaching a fork - one part of the path turns left, and the other turns right. Each looks exactly the same: tall lush trees, bright blue skies, colorful flowers, birds chirping, smiling people, and benches to sit on. However, as you walk down the path to the left, you walk straight ahead. You'd like to stop, chat with people, soak in the sunshine, sit, relax, and enjoy the scenery, but you don't. Instead, you keep going and going, head down, never stopping to rest, chat, or look around. The hours seem like years by the time you reach the end. What do you see when you get to the end of this path? What do you look like? How do you feel?

Now, imagine you walk down the path on the right. Along this route, you wave to those passing by. Sometimes you stop to chat and laugh for a while. You smile as you walk with your head up to the sky. The sun warms your face as you lean back on a bench listening to birdsongs and smelling the wildflowers. Sadly, you reach the end of the path. What do you see? What do you look like? How do you feel?

Choose self-neglect, and find yourself heading left. Choose self-care, and find yourself heading right. **Dear Caregiver**, you get to choose your path.

I've been in your shoes, and I see you. I appreciate all you are doing. Please know you are not the only one in this caregiving experience. It's common and natural to feel stressed. But please also know that you don't deserve to suffer, nor do you have to.

When you suffer, your loved one suffers. When you suffer, they lose your ability to care for them. When you hear yourself saying, "I don't have time for this," or "I have too much going on to think about myself," you're already knocking on burnout's door. Let these words act as your trigger. The triggers that tell you to take care of yourself and fast. You deserve peace and health in your body and mind, heart and soul.

In this book, I've given you tips, strategies, and techniques to practice self-care. Now you get to personalize them. Turn them into what you might call your very own 'Stress Relief Toolkit.' It's impossible to escape stress entirely, but by incorporating simple acts of self-care, you *can* find balance and help save yourself from burnout. Get back to living for *you* again. When you do this, you show up a better version of yourself, embrace life with more joy, and in turn, find ways to be a better caregiver.

Dear Caregiver,

The most important relationship in life is the one you have with yourself. So it's time to start treating yourself like the most important person.

PLEASE SHARE

If you found this book helpful in any way, big or small, I would greatly appreciate you leaving a review and providing feedback. With the knowledge and information provided in this tip-book, I hope you will find your most balanced and authentic you. I invite you to leave a review, share your thoughts, and let me know how else I may help you. If you believe this guidebook might help someone else, please share it with your friends, family, and community.

Please know you are not alone in this caregiving journey. We have an entire community to support you. If you would like to hear more from me, I'd love to connect with you. Follow me on Facebook and Instagram or join my email list.

Join our Facebook Community Death.Care.Coach

Facebook Community Group: https://www.facebook.com/groups/death.care.coach

Instagram: @death.care.coach

Webpage: www.deathcarecoach.com

BONUS
Your Grief Your Way

"Grieving doesn't make you imperfect. It makes you human."

- Sarah Dessen

Grief. A simple word yet complex in its meaning. It stems from the French term, *grever*, which means to burden, and is defined today as a "deep sorrow." While most of us often associate grief with the death of a loved one, in reality, we experience grief with any loss, change, or, as the French put it, burden. As a caregiver, you will likely experience some form of grief, which is completely normal. In many ways, it's expected. Your life is different now and probably unexpectedly different. You might experience disbelief or denial, anger or sadness, depression or anxiety, blame or shame, or others. It's common and natural to miss and grieve the loss of your old life - your life *before* caregiving. You will experience this loss in your own personal way, never to be compared or judged. Your grief and the ways you express it are entirely valid. There is no reason to be guilty, ashamed, or apologetic for your grief response.

Disenfranchised grief is a term that describes a "loss that is not openly acknowledged, socially mourned, or publicly supported." This type of grief leaves us feeling unentitled to our natural emotions. From divorce to the loss of a job. From the birth of your first child to moving to a new home after 25 years. Similar to becoming a caregiver, anytime our life changes, we grieve. And it's totally okay, normal, natural, and legitimate!

So don't dismiss your feelings. Instead, acknowledge the loss of your old life and honor what it means to you. Then, through journaling, support groups, therapists, or creating new rituals, explore ways to express, mourn, and process your loss.

Dear Caregiver,
Honor your right to grieve.

Acknowledgments

"And once the storm is over, you won't remember how you made it through, how you managed to survive. You won't even be sure, whether the storm is really over. But one thing is certain. When you come out of the storm, you won't be the same person who walked in. That's what this storm's all about."

- Haruki Murakami

I want to take the time to acknowledge all the caregivers who dedicate their lives to caring for others. Day-in and day-out, you show up. You are selfless. You are compassionate. You are *so* giving. It's been my honor to work side by side with so many of you. I know how much you do. I know how much you sacrifice. I know how unbelievably hard you work, and yet, every day, you find a way to keep moving forward. You do what you have to do. I want to thank you for who you are and all you take on. You truly are the unsung heroes of this world. I'm not sure how we'd survive without you. So, sincerely, from my heart, thank you. This book is for you. I hope it will give you hope and sanity, helping you find your way back to your most authentic you.

About the Author

Katie Duncan, MSN, CRNP, AGPCNP-BC, is a national board-certified nurse practitioner, educator, author, and death coach with a vision to rid society's stigma of death and dying. She is a practicing adult-gerontology primary care nurse practitioner and a former full-time professor at Drexel University. She is the founder and CEO of Death Care Coach, a company offering end-of-life guidance, consulting, education, and coaching to families, caregivers, and healthcare providers.

Katie has worked in healthcare in various roles and diverse specialties. She spent time in hospital and intensive care settings. She has also worked in home-care and community settings, navigating her way into diverse homes while developing strong, trusting relationships with her patients and their families. In addition, Katie has spent time in sub-acute rehab, assisted living, independent living, nursing home, and long-term care facilities. Of all the places Katie has worked, her greatest love has always been end-of-life hospice care. It has been her honor to be at the bedside of her precious fellow humans as they take their last breaths in their physical bodies. Her journey has taught her the precious gift life offers and the opportunity to see beauty at the end of every life. Katie has made it her mission to educate, coach, and provide holistic services focusing on end-of-life matters.

ALSO BY KATIE DUNCAN

The Dying Process

Your Essential Guide To Understanding Signs, Symptoms & Changes At The End Of Life

Paperback, eBook, and Audible Available on Amazon

THE CRUCIAL TOOLKIT
FOR END-OF-LIFE CARE

Get Your Exclusive Copy Now!

In the Crucial Toolkit For End-Of-Life Care, you'll learn...

- The 7 most important medications used at the end-of-life and why

- The 4 most essential and easy to use templates to keep every caregiver organized
- The simplest guide to understanding your hospice professional team members
- The 5 best questions to ask your healthcare team when caring for someone at the end-of-life

Insert link in browser:

www.deathcarecoach.com

REFERENCES

11 INSPIRATIONAL QUOTES ABOUT ORGANIZATION. (2022). The Order Expert.
https://www.theorderexpert.com/11-inspirational-quotes-about-organization/

60 Small Victories Quotes To Motivate You Everyday. (2021, May 15). Quotes Vibes. https://quotesvibes.com/small-victories-quotes/

65 Best "Asking For Help" Quotes To Guide You. (2022, July 8). Kidadl. https://kidadl.com/quotes/best-asking-for-help-quotes-to-guide-you

68 Accountability Quotes - Inspirational Words of Wisdom. (n.d.). Wow4u. https://www.wow4u.com/accountable-quotes/

150 "Good Morning" Quotes to Start Your Day — Rise & Shine! (2022, July 1). Parade: Entertainment, Recipes, Health, Life, Holidays. https://parade.com/936820/parade/good-morning-quotes/

A Beautiful Thing Is Never Perfect. (2020, September 21). Tiny Buddha. https://tinybuddha.com/blog/a-beautiful-thing-is-never-perfect/

Alicia Keys Quotes. (n.d.). BrainyQuote. https://www.brainyquote.com/quotes/alicia_keys_390562?src=t_bathroom+

AMA releases new physician guide on caring for the caregiver. (2018). AMA Press Releases.

https://www.ama-assn.org/press-center/press-releases/ama-releases-new-physician-guide-caring-caregiver

Andersen, C. H. (2022, March 16). *16 Quotes About Boundaries That Will Help You Say "No."* The Healthy. https://www.thehealthy.com/mental-health/boundaries-quotes/

A quote by Gautama Buddha. (n.d.). Goodreads. *https://www.goodreads.com/quotes/7773216-to-keep-the-body-in-good-health-is-a-duty*

A quote by Haruki Murakami. (n.d.). Goodreads. https://www.goodreads.com/quotes/315361-and-once-the-storm-is-over-you-won-t-remember-how

A quote by Jim Rohn. (n.d.). Goodreads. *https://www.goodreads.com/quotes/9042090-take-care-of-your-body-it-s-the-only-place-you*

A quote by John C. Maxwell. (n.d.). Goodreads. *https://www.goodreads.com/quotes/2312803-you-ll-never-change-your-life-until-you-change-something-you*

A quote by Lao Tzu. (n.d.). Goodreads. *https://www.goodreads.com/quotes/523350-if-you-are-depressed-you-are-living-in-the-past*

A quote by Reinhold Niebuhr. (n.d.). Goodreads. *https://www.goodreads.com/quotes/38858-god-grant-me-the-serenity-to-accept-the-things-i*

A quote by Sean Patrick Flanery. (n.d.). Goodreads. *https://www.goodreads.com/quotes/7022248-do-something-today-that-your-future-self-will-thank-you*

A quote from Daring Greatly. (n.d.). Goodreads. *https://www.goodreads.com/quotes/8955590-connection-is-why-we-re-here-we-are-hardwired-to-connect*

A quote from The Truth About Forever. (n.d.). Goodreads. *https://www.goodreads.com/quotes/194058-grieving-doesn-t-make-you-imperfect-it-makes-you-human*

Asking For Help Quotes (31 quotes). (n.d.). Goodreads. https://www.goodreads.com/quotes/tag/asking-for-help

Avendaño, K. (2022, April 6). *60 Best Nature Quotes That Capture the Beauty of the Outdoors.* Good Housekeeping. https://www.goodhousekeeping.com/life/g39478025/nature-quotes/?slide=25

Barkley, S. (2022, March 7). *15 Quotes to Help You Deal Only with What You CAN Control.* Power of Positivity: Positive Thinking & Attitude. https://www.powerofpositivity.com/what-you-can-control-quotes/

Benefits for caregivers. (2014). Government of Canada, Financial Consumer Agency.

https://www.canada.ca/en/financial-consumer-agency/services/caring-someone-ill/benefits-tax-credits-caregivers.html

Benefits of Exercise. (2022). UK National Health Service.

https://www.nhs.uk/live-well/exercise/easy-low-impact-exercises/

Bhatt, A. (2020, October 8). *50 Asking For Help Quotes To Inspire You.* The Random Vibez. https://www.therandomvibez.com/asking-for-help-quotes/

Brown, S. (2021, December 15). *Lubricant: Russell Howard's "brilliant" Netflix special is "best thing fans have watched."* Bristol-Live. https://www.bristolpost.co.uk/news/celebs-tv/lubricant-russell-howards-brilliant-netflix-6352493

Buijze, G.A., Sierevelt, I.N., Van der Heijden, B.C.J., Dijkgraaf, M.G., and Frings-Dresen, M.H.W. (2016). *The Effect of Cold Showering on Health and Work: A Randomized Controlled Trial,* NIH National Library of Medicine, 11(9): e0161749. https://www.ncbi.nlm.nih.gov/pmc/articles/PMC5025014/

Can I Get Paid to Be a Caregiver for a Family Member? (2021). AARP.

https://www.aarp.org/caregiving/financial-legal/info-2017/you-can-get-paid-as-a-family-caregiver.html

Cardoza, K., & Schneider, C. M. (2021, June 14). *The Importance Of Mourning Losses (Even When They Seem Small).* NPR.org. https://www.npr.org/2021/06/02/1002446604/the-importance-of-mourning-losses-even-when-they-seem-small

Caregiver Burnout: Steps for Coping With Stress. (2021). AARP.

https://www.aarp.org/caregiving/life-balance/info-2018/stress-management-tips.html

Caregiving Resource Center. (2020, May 29). Caring.com. https://www.caring.com/caregivers/

Carer's Allowance – How it works. (2022). GOV.UK. https://www.gov.uk/carers-allowance

Caring for the Caregiver.(2022). National Cancer Institute. https://www.cancer.gov/publications/patient-education/caring-for-the-caregiver.pdf

Cirino, E. (2019, April 18). *10 Tips to Help You Stop Ruminating.* Healthline. https://www.healthline.com/health/how-to-stop-ruminating#tips

Conley, M. (2022, March 28). *45 Quotes That Celebrate Teamwork, Hard Work, and Collaboration.* https://blog.hubspot.com/marketing/teamwork-quotes

Cory Allen (@HeyCoryAllen) /. (2022, September 10). Twitter. https://twitter.com/heycoryallen

Creswell, J.D., Dutcher, J.M., Klein, Wm. M.P., Harris, P.R., Levine, J.M. (2013). *Self-Affirmation Improves Problem-Solving under Stress*, National Library of Medicine, 8(5): e62593. https://www.ncbi.nlm.nih.gov/pmc/articles/PMC3641050/

Cullen, M. (2020). *How to Regulate Your Emotions Without Suppressing Them*, Greater Good Magazine. https://greatergood.berkeley.edu/article/
item/how_to_regulate_your_emotions_without_suppressing_them

Curiosity Quotes (1167 quotes). (n.d.). Goodreads. https://www.goodreads.com/quotes/tag/curiosity

Dahl, D. L. C. (2022, September 3). *'How to Adapt' Quotes That Can Help You Through Tough Times.* Everyday Power. https://everydaypower.com/how-to-adapt-quotes/

Dave Barry Quote. (n.d.). A-Z Quotes. https://www.azquotes.com/quote/365497

Deepak Chopra - No matter what the situation, remind yourself. . . I have a choice. (2021, April 26). The Best Famous Quotes & Sayings at Ezuie.com. https://ezuie.com/quotes/deepak-chopra-221/

Delagran, L., MA, Med, *What Is Spirituality?* (2022). Taking Charge of your Health & Wellbeing. Univ. of Minnesota. https://www.takingcharge.csh.umn.edu/what-spirituality

Diaphragmatic Breathing. (2022). Cleveland Clinic. https://my.clevelandclinic.org/health/articles/9445-diaphragmatic-breathing

Digestive Health Team. (2021, December 27). *Is Being 'Hangry' Really a Thing — or Just an Excuse?* Cleveland Clinic. https://health.clevelandclinic.org/is-being-hangry-really-a-thing-or-just-an-excuse/

Digital Detox Quotes (16 quotes). (n.d.). Goodreads. https://www.goodreads.com/quotes/tag/digital-detox

Duncan, K. (2021, September 20). *The Dying Process: Your Essential Guide To Understanding Signs, Symptoms & Changes At The End Of Life.* Independently published.

Edberg, H. (2022, May 4). *71 Self Care Quotes to Help You to Take Care of Yourself.* The Positivity Blog. https://www.positivityblog.com/self-care-quotes/

Edemekong, P.F.; Bomgaars, D.L.; Sukumaran, S.; Schoo, C. (2022). *Activities of Daily Living*, NIH National Library of Medicine. https://www.ncbi.nlm.nih.gov/books/NBK470404/

Edmund Burke Quotes. (n.d.). BrainyQuote. https://www.brainyquote.com/quotes/edmund_burke_125312

Education Quotes. (2022). Brainy Quote. https://www.brainyquote.com/topics/education-quotes

Exercise Quotes (459 quotes). (n.d.). Goodreads. https://www.goodreads.com/quotes/tag/exercise

Facial Cleanliness. (2022). Water, Sanitation, and Environmentally Related Hygiene (WASH). CDC Centers for Disease Control and Prevention. https://www.cdc.gov/healthywater/hygiene/face/index.html

Family and Medical Leave (FMLA). (2022). U.S. Dept. of Labor. https://www.dol.gov/general/topic/benefits-leave/fmla

Florence Littauer Quote. (n.d.). Quote Fancy. https://quotefancy.com/quote/1718015/Florence-Littauer-The-beauty-of-the-written-word-is-that-it-can-be-held-close-to-the

Geiger, E. (2018, July 9). *You Are Only as Strong as Your Foundation*. Eric Geiger. *https://ericgeiger.com/2012/10/you-are-only-as-strong-as-your-foundation/*

Gibby-Brown, S. (2022, September 13). *50 Inspirational Bob Proctor Quotes That Will Help You Transform Your Life*. Everyday Power. *https://everydaypower.com/bob-proctor-quotes/*

Give your brain a break. (2020, November 14). Winnipeg Free Press. https://www.winnipegfreepress.com/arts-and-life/life/2020/11/14/give-your-brain-a-break-2

Goto, Y., Hayasaka, S., Kurihara, S., & Nakamura, Y. (2018). Physical and Mental Effects of Bathing: A Randomized Intervention Study. *Evidence-based complementary and alternative medicine* : eCAM, 2018, 9521086. https://doi.org/10.1155/2018/9521086

Goyal, M., Singh, S., Sibinga, E. M. S., Gould, N. F., Rowland-Seymour, A., Sharma, R., Berger, Z., Sleicher, D., Maron, D. D., Shihab, H. M., Ranasinghe, P. D., Linn, S., Saha, S., Bass, E. B., & Haythornthwaite, J. A. (2014, March 1). *Meditation Programs for Psychological Stress and Well-being*. JAMA Internal Medicine, 174(3), 357. https://doi.org/10.1001/jamainternmed.2013.13018

Gratitude Quotes (2179 quotes). (n.d.). Goodreads. https://www.goodreads.com/quotes/tag/gratitude

Harvard Health. (2021, August 14). *Giving thanks can make you happier*. https://www.health.harvard.edu/healthbeat/giving-thanks-can-make-you-happier

Health Quality Ontario. (2022). *Palliative Care: Care for Adults With a Progressive, Life-Limiting Illness*. https://www.hqontario.ca/Evidence-to-Improve-Care/Quality-Standards/View-all-Quality-Standards/Palliative-Care/Quality-Statement-9-Caregiver-Support

Hirshkowitz, M., Whiton, K., Albert, S.M., Alessi, C., Bruni, O., et. al.; Paruthi, S., Brooks, L.J., D'Ambrosio, C., Hall, W.A., Kotagal, S., Lloyd, R.M., et al.; Watson, N.F., Badr, M.S., Belenky, G., et. al. (2017). *How Much Sleep Do I Need?* Sleep and Sleep Disorders. CDC Centers for Disease Control and Prevention. https://www.cdc.gov/sleep/about_sleep/how_much_sleep.html

How To Get Paid By The State For Taking Care Of Someone: 3

Benefits Programs. (2022).   Daily Caring. https://dailycaring.com/
getting-paid-as-a-family-caregiver-3-government-benefits-programs/

How to Shift Your Perspective to Have a Positive Outlook - 2022.
(2021, May 26). MasterClass. https://www.masterclass.com/articles/
how-to-shift-your-perspective-to-have-a-positive-outlook

Insurgent Quotes by Veronica Roth(page 9 of 24). (n.d.).
Goodreads.   https://www.goodreads.com/work/quotes/15524542-
insurgent

Is It Normal to Think About Sex a Lot? (2021, November 13). Isha.
https://isha.sadhguru.org/in/en/wisdom/article/sex-is-it-normal-to-
think-a-lot

Jacob, C. (2022, January 5). *The 50 [BEST] Quotes on Respect (in
2022)*. UpJourney. https://upjourney.com/respect-quotes

John Lubbock Quotes (Author of The Pleasures of Life). (n.d.).
Goodreads.   https://www.goodreads.com/author/quotes/
415473.John_Lubbock

Katherine, A. (2022). *Boundaries: Where You End and I Begin*,
Violence Intervention and Prevention Center, Univ. of Kentucky.
https://www.uky.edu/hr/sites/www.uky.edu.hr/files/wellness/
images/Conf14_Boundaries.pdf

Larson, E. (2001) \. Columbia Univ. School of Nursing, *Hygiene of
the Skin: When Is Clean Too Clean?* Emerging Infectious Diseases,
CDC Centers for Disease Control and Prevention.
   https://wwwnc.cdc.gov/eid/article/7/2/70-0225_article

LeaMond, N. (2021). *New RAISE Report Outlines 5 Goals to
Improve Lives of Family Caregivers*, AARP. https://www.aarp.org/
caregiving/basics/info-2021/raise-report.html?
intcmp=AE-CAR-BB

Let my people glo   (@MichellCClark) /. (2021, November 12).
Twitter. https://mobile.twitter.com/MichellCClark

Liles, M. (2022, July 1). *Say "Cheese!" 150 Uplifting Smile
Quotes That'll Get You Grinning From Ear to Ear*. Parade: Entertainment, Recipes, Health, Life, Holidays. https://parade.com/.amp/
1045449/marynliles/smile-quotes/.

Ludlam, J. (2022, February 11). *30 Self Love Quotes that Celebrate the Greatness of You*. Country Living. https://www.countryliving.com/life/g29661464/self-love-quotes/

Mackey, M. (2022, July 1). *100 Quotes About Self-Care, Because Being Good to Yourself Has Never Been More Important*. Parade: Entertainment, Recipes, Health, Life, Holidays. https://parade.com/1070248/maureenmackey/self-care-quotes/

Mahoney, K. D. (n.d.). *Latin Definition for: gratia, gratiae (ID: 21673) - Latin Dictionary and Grammar Resources - Latdict*. https://latin-dictionary.net/definition/21673/gratia-gratiae

Mark Twain Quote. (n.d.). A-Z Quotes. https://www.azquotes.com/quote/572327

Martinez, N. L. C. (2022, August 29). *Letting Go Quotes For Finally Moving On*. Everyday Power. https://everydaypower.com/letting-go-quotes/

Mayo Clinic Staff. (2022). *Mindfulness exercises*. Consumer Health. https://www.mayoclinic.org/healthy-lifestyle/consumer-health/in-depth/mindfulness-exercises/art-20046356

McDonald, J. N. (2022, August 3). *30+ Motivational Quotes for Students*. Southern Living. https://www.southernliving.com/culture/school/motivational-quotes-for-students

McGlone, F., Walker, S. (2021, June 22). *Four Ways Hugs Are Good for Your Health*, Greater Good Magazine. https://greatergood.berkeley.edu/article/item/four_ways_hugs_are_good_for_your_health

Meah, A. (2022). *34 Inspirational Quotes On Choices*, Awaken the Greatness Within. https://www.awakenthegreatnesswithin.com/34-inspirational-quotes-choices/

Meah, A. (2018, September 29). *35 Inspirational Quotes On Self-Forgiveness*. AwakenTheGreatnessWithin. https://www.awakenthegreatnesswithin.com/35-inspirational-quotes-on-self-forgiveness/

Meah, A. (2019, January 29). *35 Inspirational Quotes On Failure*. AwakenTheGreatnessWithin. https://www.awakenthegreatnesswithin.com/35-inspirational-quotes-on-failure/

Medrut, F. (2020, November 25). *25 Self-Care Quotes That Will Encourage You To Treat Yourself Better*. Goalcast. https://www.goalcast.com/self-care-quotes/

Melissa Steginus Quotes (Author of Everyday Mindfulness). (n.d.). Goodreads. https://www.goodreads.com/author/quotes/19611101.Melissa_Steginus

Mobbs, C. H. (2019, December 21). *Perspective and perception*. ExpatChild. https://expatchild.com/quotes-perspective-perception/

Mollaioli, D., Sansone, A., Ciocca, G., Limoncin, E., Colonnello, E., Di Lorenzo, G., & Jannini, E. A. (2021, January). Benefits of Sexual Activity on Psychological, Relational, and Sexual Health During the COVID-19 Breakout. *The Journal of Sexual Medicine*, *18*(1), 35–49. https://doi.org/10.1016/j.jsxm.2020.10.008

Newhouse, L. L. (2021, March 1). *Is crying good for you?* Harvard Health. https://www.health.harvard.edu/blog/is-crying-good-for-you-2021030122020

Norbert Juma, Lead Editor. (2022, September 6). *Trust Quotes Honoring Confidence, Belief and Faith*. Everyday Power. https://everydaypower.com/trust-quotes/

Pajer, N. (2022, July 1). *Quiet the Mind and Get Your Zen on With These 50 Quotes About Meditation*. Parade: Entertainment, Recipes, Health, Life, Holidays. https://parade.com/1066461/nicolepajer/meditation-quotes/

Pangilinan, J. (2022, February 24). *41 Inspiring & Powerful Quotes About Community to Help Others [2022]*. Happier Human. https://www.happierhuman.com/community-quotes/

Pangilinan, J. (2022, February 24). *91 Spiritual Quotes to Awaken and Enrich Your Life*. Happier Human. https://www.happierhuman.com/spiritual-quotes/

Pope, K. (2021, November 23). *50 Self-Love Quotes to Boost Your Confidence and Lift Your Spirits*. Good Housekeeping. https://www.goodhousekeeping.com/life/g38333580/self-love-quotes/

Positive Affirmation Quotes (343 quotes). (n.d.). Goodreads. https://www.goodreads.com/quotes/tag/positive-affirmation

Positive Self Talk Quotes & Sayings. (2021, September 22). The Goal Chaser. https://thegoalchaser.com/positive-self-talk-quotes/

Powell, A. (2018). *When Science Meets Mindfulness.* Health & Medicine. *The Harvard Gazette.* https://www.geisinger.org/health-and-wellness/wellness-articles/2018/03/29/21/13/stop-holding-it-in-4-bodily-functions-you-should-let-out

Price-Mitchell, M., PhD. (2020, December 18). *Quotes About Curiosity That Inspire Kids' Life-Long Learning.* Roots of Action. https://www.rootsofaction.com/quotes-about-curiosity/

Ray Charles Quotes (Author of Brother Ray). (n.d.). Goodreads. https://www.goodreads.com/author/quotes/272011.Ray_Charles

Sager, J. (2022, September 5). *100 Inspirational Quotes to Keep You Inspired in 2022—You Can Do Hard Things!* Parade: Entertainment, Recipes, Health, Life, Holidays. https://parade.com/973277/jessicasager/inspirational-quotes/

Sansone, R. A., & Sansone, L. A. (2012). Rumination: relationships with physical health. *Innovations in clinical neuroscience, 9*(2), 29–34.

Zamani Sani, S. H., Fathirezaie, Z., Brand, S., Pühse, U., Holsboer-Trachsler, E., Gerber, M., & Talepasand, S. (2016). Physical activity and self-esteem: testing direct and indirect relationships associated with psychological and physical mechanisms. *Neuropsychiatric disease and treatment, 12*, 2617–2625. https://doi.org/10.2147/NDT.S116811

Sansone, R.A., MD, Sansone, L.A., MD. (2010). *Gratitude and Well Being*, National Library of Medicine, (11): 18–22. https://www.ncbi.nlm.nih.gov/pmc/articles/PMC3010965/

Say, J. (2020, April 15). *44 Journaling Quotes (BENEFITS OF JOURNALING).* Gracious Quotes. https://graciousquotes.com/journaling-quotes/

Sayings, G. (n.d.). *Fuel Your Body Quotes: top 57 famous sayings about Fuel Your Body.* https://www.greatsayings.net/sayings-about-fuel-your-body/

Self Identification Quotes (16 quotes). (n.d.). Goodreads. https://www.goodreads.com/quotes/tag/self-identification

Shakti Gawain Quotes. (n.d.). BrainyQuote. https://www.brainyquote.com/quotes/shakti_gawain_390054

Sharma, S. (2021, November 28). *Top 10 Togetherness Quotes | For Your Loved Once.* Republic Quote. https://republicquote.com/togetherness-quotes/

Smith, M., M.A. (2022). *Caregiver Stress and Burnout.* Help Guide. https://www.helpguide.org/articles/stress/caregiver-stress-and-burnout.htm

Somatic Mental Health. (n.d.). Embodied Therapy. https://www.embodied-therapy.com/

Some Activity is Better than None. (2022). Physical Activity, Adults. CDC Centers for Disease Control and Prevention. https://www.cdc.gov/physicalactivity/basics/adults/index.htm

Staff, H. B. (2022, June 18). *The 87 Greatest Fashion Quotes of All Time.* Harper's BAZAAR. https://www.harpersbazaar.com/fashion/designers/a1576/50-famous-fashion-quotes/

Suciu, P. (2021, June 24). *Americans Spent On Average More Than 1,300 Hours On Social Media Last Year.* Forbes. https://www.forbes.com/sites/petersuciu/2021/06/24/americans-spent-more-than-1300-hours-on-social-media/?sh=7c85e6892547

Taking Care of Yourself: Tips for Caregivers. (2017). National Institute on Aging. https://www.nia.nih.gov/health/taking-care-yourself-tips-caregivers

Tips for Better Sleep. (2016). Sleep and Sleep Disorders. CDC Centers for Disease Control and Prevention. https://www.cdc.gov/sleep/about_sleep/sleep_hygiene.html

Terzakis, BSN, RN, MacKenzie, PhD, RN. (2019). *Preparing Family Members for the Death of a Loved One in Long-Term Care,* Annals of Long-Term Care. https://www.hmpgloballearningnetwork.com/site/altc/articles/preparing-family-members-death-loved-one-long-term-care

The Benefits of a Healthy Sex Life | Center for Women's Health |

OHSU. (n.d.). https://www.ohsu.edu/womens-health/benefits-healthy-sex-life

The Benefits of Slumber. (2013). NIH News in Health. https://newsinhealth.nih.gov/2013/04/benefits-slumber

The Editors at Chopra.com. (2021, August 6). *How Breathwork Benefits the Mind, Body, and Spirit*. Chopra. https://chopra.com/articles/how-breathwork-benefits-the-mind-body-and-spirit

The Health Benefits of Smiling. (2018). SCL Health. https://www.sclhealth.org/blog/2019/06/the-real-health-benefits-of-smiling-and-laughing/

The importance of hydration,. (2017). Harvard T.H. Chan School of Public Health.
https://www.hsph.harvard.edu/news/hsph-in-the-news/the-importance-of-hydration/

The Power of Community Quotes. (2021, February 3). Ellevate. https://www.ellevatenetwork.com/articles/8538-quotes-about-the-power-of-community

The Power of No Quotes by James Altucher. (n.d.). Goodreads. https://www.goodreads.com/work/quotes/26342007-the-power-of-no-because-one-little-word-can-bring-health-abundance-an

The Stages of Grief: Accepting the Unacceptable. (2020, June 8). Counseling Center. https://www.washington.edu/counseling/2020/06/08/the-stages-of-grief-accepting-the-unacceptable/

Tom Brady Quotes. (n.d.). BrainyQuote. https://www.brainyquote.com/quotes/tom_brady_806988

Tony Robbins Quotes. (n.d.). BrainyQuote. https://www.brainyquote.com/quotes/tony_robbins_132532

TOP 25 ASKING FOR HELP QUOTES. (n.d.). A-Z Quotes. https://www.azquotes.com/quotes/topics/asking-for-help.html

Wang, S. S. (2015, August 10). *Worrying About the Future, Ruminating on the Past—How Thoughts Affect Mental Health*. WSJ. https://www.wsj.com/articles/worrying-about-the-future-ruminating-on-the-pasthow-thoughts-affect-mental-health-1439223597

Watson, L.R., MSN RN, Fraser, M., MSN RN, Ballas, P, MD.

(2022). *Journaling for Mental Health*, Univ. Of Rochester Medical Center, Health Encyclopedia.

https://www.urmc.rochester.edu/encyclopedia/content.aspx? ContentID=4552&ContentTypeID=1

Werner, S.A., MD. (2018). *Stop holding it in! 4 bodily functions you should let out*, Geisinger Health. https://www.geisinger.org/health-and-wellness/wellness-articles/2018/03/29/21/13/stop-holding-it-in-4-bodily-functions-you-should-let-out

What Can Adults Do to Maintain Good Oral Health? (2021). Oral Health Tips. CDC Centers for Disease Control and Prevention. https:// www.cdc.gov/oralhealth/basics/adult-oral-health/tips.html

What Happens to the Brain in Alzheimer's Disease? (n.d.). National Institute on Aging. https://www.nia.nih.gov/health/what-happens-brain-alzheimers-disease

What Is Respite Care? (2022). NIH National Institute on Aging. https://www.nia.nih.gov/health/what-respite-care

What is stress? (2021). UK Mental Health Foundation. https:// www.mentalhealth.org.uk/a-to-z/s/stress

Why breakfast is so important. (2022). Better Health Channel. https://www.betterhealth.vic.gov.au/health/healthyliving/breakfast

Williams A. M. (2018). Education, Training, and Mentorship of Caregivers of Canadians Experiencing a Life-Limiting Illness. *Journal of palliative medicine*, *21*(S1), S45–S49. https://doi.org/10. 1089/jpm.2017.0393

Wim Hof Quote: But, there is still every reason for healthy people to take cold showers, or swim outside in cold water. (n.d.). Quote Fancy. https://quotefancy.com/quote/2836588/Wim-Hof-But-there-is-still-every-reason-for-healthy-people-to-take-cold-showers-or-swim

Winston Churchill Quotes. (n.d.). BrainyQuote. https://www. brainyquote.com/quotes/winston_churchill_103788

Ma, X., Yue, Z. Q., Gong, Z. Q., Zhang, H., Duan, N. Y., Shi, Y. T., Wei, G. X., & Li, Y. F. (2017). The Effect of Diaphragmatic Breathing on Attention, Negative Affect and Stress in Healthy Adults. *Frontiers in psychology*, *8*, 874. https://doi.org/10.3389/fpsyg.2017.00874

You Are Not Alone Quotes (15 quotes). (n.d.). Goodreads. https://www.goodreads.com/quotes/tag/you-are-not-alone

Zaccaro, A., Piarulli, A., Laurino, M., Garbella, E., Menicucci, D., Neri, B., & Gemignani, A. (2018). How Breath-Control Can Change Your Life: A Systematic Review on Psycho-Physiological Correlates of Slow Breathing. *Frontiers in human neuroscience, 12,* 353. https://doi.org/10.3389/fnhum.2018.00353

Zone, R. T. (2022, August 23). *99 Best Quotes About Breathing (Respiratory Therapist Edition).* Respiratory Therapy Zone. https://www.respiratorytherapyzone.com/quotes-about-breathing/